The Ideal *"I Do"*

Pursuing the Marriage You'll Love

Book 1: Building Strong

By Dr. Dave Currie & Jody Wandzura

Want to be ready for a great marriage? Of course, you do! Join this father-daughter expert tandem on your journey to an amazing relationship. Combined, they have coached nearly 800 couples to date in premarital preparation. Anchored by a vibrant faith in God and a deep belief in the beauty of marriage, they will help you navigate the best track to the top of the marital mountain. In their straight-shooting and practical approach, they powerfully outline all the significant steps enroute to the most amazing start for your marital climb toward *The Ideal "I Do"*!

Overcoming Grouse Grind

Why This Pre-Marriage/New Marriage Series:

A Solid, Practical Guidebook
- A complete, doable, sensible marital game plan,
- Thorough coverage of all key and relevant marriage topics
- Short chapters designed for quick "in and out" reads
- Interactive questions designed for helpful discussion

Professional, Experienced Advice
- Coaching from authors with massive pre-marital experience
- Perspective from two different generations
- Authors still *'in the trenches'* teaching and counseling
- Authors have traveled extensively speaking together

Summiting Mt. Baker in a Snowstorm

Genuine, Well-Researched Experts
- 19 years of post-secondary education combined
- Reflecting the current "best practices" for a great marriage
- Dr. Dave is a veteran, clinical therapist
- Jody's Master's project assessed 40+ premarital resources

Reassuring Hope for Your Marriage
- Anchored by timeless truths coming from a deep, vibrant faith in God
- Marital help that will save you a boatload of hurt and regret
- A very readable, comprehendible and sensible guide
- Hope for achieving a strong start in your marriage

Enjoying Black Tusk

Read On for the Best Marital Journey Possible!

What people are saying about The Ideal *"I Do"*

"This new marriage series, based on a solid Biblical and theological foundation, is combined with immense practical applications. Written by two friends who I admire greatly for both their Christlikeness and their commitment to families, their books will coach you, challenge you, and make you a better marriage partner."

Dr. Stephen J. Bramer
Chair and Professor of Bible Exposition, Dallas Theological Seminary
Teaching Pastor at Waterbrook Bible Fellowship, Wylie, Texas.

"People often enter marriage with good intentions, passionate hearts, foggy lens...and more than a few secrets and hidden pain. Dr. Dave Currie and Jody Wandzura have spent decades restoring hearts and helping marriages thrive. They have helped thousands of marital train wrecks get back on track. In The Ideal "I Do" series, Currie and Wandzura are determined to help couples start well, so they can share lives that are filled with fun, joy, wholeness, transparency, and God's unfailing love. They take you on a fearless and intentional journey to ignite true and Godly passion for one another."

Sam Black
Director of Recovery Education
Covenant Eyes, Owosso, Michigan

"I have known Dr. Dave for over 4 decades and have personally benefited from his immense wisdom and experience on 'all things' marriage. I expect there are few, if anyone in Canada, with more firsthand experience on this topic. Dave & Jody's companion set will surely become the "go-to" handbooks for anyone working in pre-marriage/new marriage counseling."

Brad Willems
Senior Financial Advisor
Assante Wealth Management, Abbotsford, BC

"I commend this awesome resource to you written by a gifted father-daughter team, the most seasoned marriage counselor Dr. Dave and his very qualified daughter, Jody. Every chapter contains inspiring insights and user-friendly applications. Created for every pre-marriage and early marriage, this is a 'must read' you will not want to miss!"

Dr. Paul Magnus
President Emeritus
Briercrest College & Seminary, Caronport, Sask.

"I have lost count of the number of couples I have referred to Dr. Dave and how many marriages he has helped dramatically — my own included. That Dave has written this resource with his daughter, Jody, is further testament to his commitment, not only as a husband, but as a father, and a man of God. I wholeheartedly endorse their book and am confident it will help engaged couples have life-long, God-honoring marriages."

Matt Shantz
Lead Pastor
Central Community Church, Chilliwack, BC

"An excellent and comprehensive work on creating a strong and lasting marriage. Their practical tools for newlyweds are exceptional for building a foundation of love to withstand future challenges."

Kirby Hanawalt
Veteran Marriage and Family Therapist
Registered Clinical Counselor/Supervisor, Richmond, BC

"The integrity and perspective that these authors bring is uncontested. Relatable, readable and anchored in living well and God's design for marriage, this book presents a refreshing, proactive approach to marriage that encourages couples to start their journey on the right foot. Short chapters are written with a light-hearted tone saturated with stabilizing principles and relevant questions that will facilitate intimate discussion toward all things that matter in both life and marriage relationships."

Dr. Heather Smith
Ministry of Education, Victoria, BC

"I've known Dr. Dave and Jody for a decade and been blessed by their lives and ministry. They are the real deal. Their authentic and sincere faith is a testimony and the foundation of this premarital/new marital resource. I highly recommend it for its wide-range of topics and practical Christian insight that outlines a great start in marriage."

Derrick Hamre
Lead Pastor
Christian Life Assembly. Langley, BC

"As Dr. Dave's accountability partner meeting weekly for over thirty years, I know for a fact that you can fully trust Dave and Jody's insights into creating a great marriage. I have. His motto of "Put God First – Life Goes Best" will come alive on each page as you "mine out" their practical relational wisdom. Know for certain, by putting God first as they suggest, your new marriage will go best."

Larry Siebert
Award-Winning Real Estate Agent
Royal LePage Little Oak Realty, Abbotsford, BC

"When it comes to beginning a lifelong, God-honoring, healthy marriage, you are holding one of the best, most practical and comprehensive books I've ever come across. Enjoy!"

Dr. Henry Schorr
Lead Pastor
Centre Street Church, Calgary, AB

"I have known Dr. Dave & Jody for over 3 decades and heard him speak many times. I know confidently that they are well-equipped to guide young couples toward God's plan for The Ideal "I Do".

Paul Henderson
Canadian Hockey Legend, Mississauga, Ont.

"If you are looking for a fantastic resource that is full of incredible content on how to build a great, new marriage, this one is a must read! Building on a solid foundation of faith, Dr. Dave and Jody share real-life stories, time-tested tools and wise principles that will make the vitally important ingredients of building a loving marriage understandable, tangible, and achievable."

Cam Broad
Life & Recovery Coach
Doing Family Right Care Centre, Abbotsford, BC

"Dr. Dave and Jody's years of counseling experience leap from the pages as they help people navigate scores of individual and relational issues in preparation for marriage. Built on the foundation of a personal faith in God, the Ideal "I Do" set will be an extraordinary tool for those planning to be married, those newly married, and frankly, even for those married a while but want to strengthen their union."

Dean Jaderston
Executive Director
Northern Pines Family Conference, Green Lake, Wisconsin

"Dr. Dave and Jody have put together a remarkable resource for young couples! Knowing them personally, I can hear their "real voices" through these chapters that are filled with Biblical wisdom and practical guidance. Any couple, at any stage of their relationship, will be challenged and blessed through these pages. If you want a deeper connection with your spouse, this series will do just that!"

Jeff Gamache
Director of Athletics
Trinity Western University, Langley, BC

"Written with a passion for God, a love for people and a desire to help marriages become strong and last long, this practical premarital series is a 'must have' resource for anyone getting married. Dr. Dave and Jody have poured out their hearts and knowledge to better equip young couples for the journey. I should know. Dave did our premarital over 40 years ago."

Darcy Kuhn
Growth & Development Pastor
Northview Community Church, Abbotsford, BC

"This amazing father-daughter duo issues a challenge for couples to roll up their sleeves, get to work and do what it takes to build a God-honoring relationship. Packed with practical tips and Christ-centered wisdom, this incredible resource offers the perfect roadmap to construct a loving, growing, grace-soaked marriage."

Debbie Tonn
Women's Pastor
Christian Life Assembly, Langley, BC

"Dr. Dave and his daughter Jody have created a fabulous marriage handbook! It is simultaneously down to earth and heavenly minded. Just like this dynamic father/daughter duo, their series is as real and practical as it is rooted in Biblical truth and lives of deep faith."

David C. Bentall
Author/Educator
Founding Principal of Next Step Advisors, Vancouver, BC

"Dr. Dave and Jody have created a very practical and applicable guide to building a God-honoring, life-giving marriage. Reading and, more importantly, working through the materials will help couples grow their marriage into what they hoped for on the day they said, "I do."

Willy Reimer
Veteran Pastor
Executive Director - 787 Collective, Calgary, AB

"Dr. Dave and Jody have provided an extensive pre-marital/new marriage pathway for those in pursuit of a deeper relational connection and a thriving future together."

Dave Klassen
National Director
Athletes in Action, Canada, Abbotsford, BC

"Dr. Dave's love for people, vast experience counseling couples and penchant for creating content to support the marital journey, make this guidebook a gem for any couple looking to get their marriage off to a great start. Partnered with his daughter Jody, their series is the perfect combination of simple, practical and profound."

Rachelle Siemens
Marriage & Family Therapist
Doing Family Right Care Centre, Surrey, BC

With Deep Gratitude

To Donalyn, my life-long companion and best friend, my faithful partner and still very much the love of my life. Thank you for so many years of joining me in opening up our lives to hundreds of starry-eyed couples to help them get a great start in their marriage. Thank you even more for allowing me to practice all my relational ideas on us. You are God's greatest gift to me. I love what we have built. Thanks for your patience and support in this project, my "latest thing".
Love, Your David.

_____

To Chris, the only person in the world I never get tired of being with. When I promised to be your *"wifee"* for as long as we both shall live, I had no idea what a deal I was getting! You have supported me in everything that I have wanted to try. You believe in me and encourage me. You have helped me persevere through the days of writer's block and editing blues. Thank you for your love and letting me share our journey of ups and downs in the writing of this book.
I love you! Jody.

_____

To Mazy and Javen, Thank you so much for your patience while I completed this book. I appreciate you for allowing me to share stories of what I have learned from you over the years. My prayer is that I will humbly follow God passionately (and my own advice in this book) so I can be a better wife for Dad and clearer example to you.
I love you both so much, Mom

WORDING DISCLAIMER: Because The Ideal "I Do" series is designed for interaction both prior to marriage and after the wedding, the term fiancé will not be used but rather partner, spouse, mate or husband and wife.

TWO BOOK RECOMMENDATION: Because The Ideal "I Do" series is designed as a workbook with projects and questions for each person throughout, it is highly recommended that both parties have a copy of the book to record their answers for the best discussion on each topic.

The Ideal "I Do"

Pursuing the Marriage You'll Love

Book 1:
Building Strong

Dr. Dave Currie
& Jody Wandzura

A Pre-Marriage/New Marriage Series

Publishing Page

The Ideal "I Do": Pursuing the Marriage You'll Love
Book 1 – Building Strong
Copyright @ 2024 1st Edition
By Dr. Dave Currie and Jody Wandzura

Published by Doing Family Right Publishing
36458 Florence Drive, Abbotsford, BC, V3G 0B6
1-604-309-6426

ISBN #978-1-0688052-0-2

Unless otherwise noted, scripture quotations are from THE HOLY BIBLE, New International Version (NIV), copyright @ 1973, 1978, 1984, 2011. Used by permission. All rights reserved.

Scripture quotations marked NLT are taken from the Holy Bible, New Living Translation, copyright@ 1996, 2004, 2007. Used by permission. All rights reserved.

Scripture quotations marked MSG are taken from The Message, copyright@ 2000, 2001, 2002. Used by permission. All rights reserved.

Scripture quotations marked TLB are taken from The Living Bible, Copyright @1971. Used by permission. All rights reserved.

Scripture quotations marked GNT are taken from The Good News Translation, Copyright @1966, 1976, 1992. Used by permission. All rights reserved.

Interior Design: Tammy Nash, Dave Currie
Cover Design: Mariah Johnson, Dave Currie, Jesse Rivas
Edited by: Tammy Nash
Author photo: Jason Brown, Revival Arts Studio

The anecdotes included in this book are a combination of our own experience and those of a composite of the many people who have participated in our premarital counseling and marriage counseling sessions over the years. To ensure privacy, names in the stories have been changed, with the exception of those used by permission. Any other similarities to a particular person are purely coincidental.

Acknowledgements

- **SPOUSES:** Dave wants to thank his wife, Donalyn Currie, of nearly fifty years for being a faithful support and constant source of joy. Jody wants to thank her husband, Chris Wandzura, for being a Godly example in both character and wisdom. We couldn't have done this without both of you!

- **MENTORS:** Dave wants to thank Larry Siebert and Paul Henderson, both modern-day patriarchs, for their years of investment into his life. He also wants to thank his parents, Ken & Dorothy Currie, for their strong example of a Jesus-filled and love-filled marriage.

  Jody wants to thank her parents (yes, that's Dr. Dave & Donalyn) for demonstrating what marriage should look like – not a perfect marriage, but a great one. She saw real life arguments followed by forgiveness, busy schedules that still made room for dates and two completely different people both fully relying on God for his guidance in their lives.

- **FRIENDS:** We send a massive thank you to Tammy Nash, extraordinary executive assistant, who single-handedly quarterbacked the editing, formatting and printing details of this book. We are indebted for your faithful, tireless and accurate work! Thank you to Mariah Johnston for consulting on the front and back covers. Finally, thank you to Laura O'Reilly and Caralee Daigle for your early assistance in content selection and initial editing.

- **COUPLES:** Thank you to the hundreds of couples who took premarital counseling from us – nearly 800 to date. We have continued to learn from you and adjust and apply our curriculum even better. Thank you also to those couples who bravely opened up about their struggles in their early years. Your heartbreak and disappointment in your unhealthy relationship fueled our desire to complete this book to help as many couples as possible get a great start to their marital life.

- **AUTHOR DEVELOPMENT COACHES:** We cannot thank Jesse and Elisheba of Above the Sun enough for the wisdom and perspective they brought as our writing advisory and publication team. They guided us so well in this project.

- **GOD:** Most of all, Dave and Jody want to thank God for His plan for marriage and for life. We have both seen that if we keep a soft heart toward God, all our relationships – especially our marriages – benefit as a result. ***Put God First – Life Goes Best!*** Thank you, Lord, for letting us be an encouragement to many young marriages.

Doing Family Right

Dr. Dave and Donalyn Currie founded Doing Family Right in 2010 as a ministry committed to helping people maximize their most important relationships – Marriage – Family – God. The website – *DoingFamilyRight.com* – has scores of resources designed to inspire family transformation. There are articles, podcasts, video teachings, a monthly E-zine, free helps and more. Check it out to be thrilled with what we offer at no cost.

Through our two Doing Family Right Care Centres, we host over 20 therapists and life coaches serving every challenge an individual, a couple or a family might face. These men and women counsel in person in the Fraser Valley in Canada or online almost anywhere. Check out the website under Care Centre to read up about the Care Team members that are available to provide help and support. You can email info@doingfamilyright.com with any questions. We love Doing Family Right... which of course is God's way.

Dr. Dave still directs DFR today – speaking, counseling and mentoring the next generation of counselors.

Table of Contents

Chapters Arranged by Theme

CHAPTER	PAGE

WORDING DISCLAIMER: Because The Ideal *"I Do"* series is designed for interaction both prior to marriage and after the wedding, the term fiancé will not be used but rather partner, spouse, mate or husband and wife.

TWO BOOK RECOMMENDATION: Because The Ideal "I Do" series is designed as a workbook with projects and questions for each person throughout, it is highly recommended that both parties have a copy of the book to record their answers for the best discussion on each topic.

How to Use The Ideal *"I Do"* Series

INVEST in your FUTURE: Make the effort toward a great start for the *"ideal"* marriage. This investment is worth your time, energy, and money! Every chapter is designed to be read, reflected upon, and discussed – **Book 1: *Building Strong*** to be completed before your wedding; **Book 2: *Lasting Long*** to take you deeper after you're married and within the first five years.

CHOOSE your OPTION:
- *Individual*: You can work through this resource by yourself in preparation for a future partner or a pending engagement.
- *Engaged Couple*: Use it once you're engaged as preparation for a strong marriage before your wedding in Book 1: *Building Strong*. There's more to come after you're married in Book 2: *Lasting Long*. Each person needs a copy.
- *Newlywed Couple:* If you are already married but want to really pursue the marriage you'll love, then dig in and enjoy both volumes. Each person needs a copy.
- *Counsellor Led:* Pastors, therapists and other marriage mentors who do premarital counseling can easily use the *Ideal "I Do"* series to anchor their ongoing marriage preparation program. See Instructions for counselors that follow.

COMPLETE your SERIES: We feel that the combination of *Book 1: Building Strong* along with *Book 2: Lasting Long* delivers the most thorough marital preparation material in existence. After working with nearly 800 couples over 40 years, it covers virtually every topic that is important to have a strong relationship. You can power through and get it done in a month, or take a chapter a week over the next year. Regardless of how long, complete both books to best prepare yourselves for **The Ideal *"I Do."***

FOLLOW the INSTRUCTIONS:
- **READ** chapters together or at least the same day to create a meaningful discussion. Underline key thoughts in your book as you read. Write in comments. Pose questions.
- **WRITE** out individual answers to the Discussion Starters at the end of each chapter. Show your commitment to your spouse by engaging fully in this preparation process.
- **DISCUSS** your perspectives while sharing your answers to the questions. Work to come to an amicable understanding.
- **CHECK** the box on the Table of Contents page for every chapter you complete together. Don't stop. Each box checked is a step toward a better marriage.
- **APPLY** what you are learning. Change takes work. Bad habits don't die easily. Commit to implementing the truths that are central to your growth as a person and a couple.
- **PRAY** asking God for help to make changes you should implement in your marriage. Get in the habit of trusting Him with the challenges you will need to work through.

TRUST in the ANCHOR: While people come from a myriad of backgrounds and faith journeys, we have found that a personal relationship with Jesus anchors who we are and how we operate. Putting God first in our lives implies making changes in how we operate – needed changes for life and marriage that are so central to having a great start. Be open to the role that you may want God to play in your new relationship moving forward.

Premarital Counselor Guidelines for The Ideal *"I Do"*

Whether you are a rookie at providing premarital counseling or a savvy veteran at helping couples to a great start, this guidebook is designed to be the complete package. We have assembled a thorough coverage of the essential and foundational components to give to any new couple. Chapters are designed as short reads for Generation Z and Generation Alpha. Book 1: *Building Strong* is premarital and Book 2: *Lasting Long* is for newlyweds.

HOW TO BEST USE THIS BOOK

1. **VIEW THE TOPICS:** Use the Chapters by Theme as your guideline for sessions (1 page back). The Major Marital Themes are:
   - *Commitment* – four chapters on prioritizing a lasting, exclusive relationship
   - *Communication* – four chapters on creating an increasing, authentic dialogue
   - *Companionship* – three chapters on targeting a delightful, deepening friendship
   - *Connection* – three chapters on maintaining a genuine, warm disposition
   - *Conflict Resolution* – three chapters on shaping productive, unifying solutions
   - *Closeness* – four chapters on developing a mutually satisfying sexual intimacy
   - *Convictions* – five chapters on embracing a vibrant life-changing faith
   - *Other Concerns* – four chapters on addressing core personal challenges

2. **PLAN THE SESSIONS:** Each theme above deserves an hour of coaching and interaction with the couple, so eight to ten hours with the couple. I usually do six sessions of ninety minutes.

3. **DIVIDE THE CONTENT:** It's up to you as to how you want to roll out the material. You choose the order and assign the chapters you'll focus on. Tailor the material to focus on issues that might be more of a challenge to the couple. Talk. Ask. Listen. Assess. Decide. Guide.

4. **ASSIGN THE CHAPTERS:**
   - **SESSION INTERACTION:** Assign chapters you will discuss during the next session. Have couples read, answer questions, discuss them at home and come prepared to interact with you about these chapters.
   - **COUPLE INTERACTION:** Assign chapters you want read and discussed before the next session. Have couples read, answer questions and discuss them for their own marital growth and benefit even though you're not covering it in session.
   - **FOLLOW-UP INTERACTION:** Remaining chapters in each section should be read and discussed by the couple for ongoing marital development. After married, encourage them to get **The Ideal *"I Do"* - Book 2: *Lasting Long*.**

5. **DISCUSS THE CHAPTERS:** Share your perspective on each chapter assigned. Personalize it with your story and experience. Take their questions on the topic. Add material that feels right to you, remembering that supplementary material, though an option, is likely unnecessary.

   NOTE: **The Ideal *"I Do"*** Series is designed as an ongoing resource like a new marriage owner's manual. Book 1: *Building Strong* for pre-marriage and Book 2: *Lasting Long* for new marriages. Encourage their completion. Consider offering a free follow-up session in the first year when they finish Book 1.

Introduction
How It All Started for Me

Dr. Dave Currie

In 1979, the movie *Kramer vs Kramer* was released by Columbia Pictures and became the highest-grossing film of that year while collecting five Academy Awards. It chronicles a marital break-up, the resulting challenges of single-parenting and then, the court battle between Ted Kramer (Dustin Hoffman) and Joanna Kramer (Meryl Streep) over the custody of their young son, Billy.

I watched the film by myself on a Sunday night after church when it aired on TV in the spring of 1982. I was 27, nearly 8 years married with 2 young kids (one was Jody, my co-author). There is no doubt that the viewing of the movie was pivotal in my journey – no, my "calling" – to start focusing on premarital preparation. You see, the trauma that was depicted in the break-up and subsequent guardianship dispute that was displayed was incredibly disturbing to my familial equilibrium. The riveting portrayal of the battle showed the deep, inner turmoil of everyone involved. I hurt. Their family breakup was so tragic and the confusion on the young boy was so, so sad.

So, yes, the movie had greatly stirred me emotionally. It still does. It had extremely impacted my own healthy family worldview as I observed so graphically the depiction of their pain. As the movie ended, I went to our piano and began playing and singing songs of faith and hope. I became teary-eyed, rocked by the reality of what goes on in some homes. Donalyn had come downstairs after putting our 2 young children to bed. She came over noticing that I was fighting tears. She asked.

It was then that I recounted the Kramer story of marital breakdown and the trauma it put the kid through. I shared how I felt it so wrong that the little guy had to suffer so much because of the selfishness of his parents. I asked her to sit down beside me on the piano bench and I remember urging her, *"Would you join me in doing what we can do in helping young marriages get a good start?"* She said she would. We held hands and I prayed as we dedicated our lives together to the building of strong marriages. That was 1982 and over 750 couples ago in premarital preparation.

But let me digress.

When I write, I speak out of our own marital brokenness. But for the grace of God, Donalyn and I could have easily been another divorce statistic. We had such relational pain. A ton of it. Our years 3 – 5, 1976-79, were difficult...really difficult. It was a dark and scary period of our lives as we had thought – or maybe assumed – our marriage would be fine. We could figure this stuff out. Well, we couldn't. Soon, our relational collisions magnified, my selfishness dominated, and the thought of separation was entertained.

We had grown so far apart that we didn't even like being together – all that in the first five years.

Looking back isn't fun. Memories of that season still bring a deep inner pain. Donalyn cried when we edited this intro chapter together. We feel our pain could have been averted if we had had some form of premarital counselling. We didn't. So, when I speak, I speak out of our own marital pain not just what I have seen in scores of other hurting marriages. I want to help you avoid all that hardship.

Our story gets crazier. You have heard it said that "God has a sense of humour." We are convinced He does. Why? It was during this broken season in our marriage that I felt 'called by God' to do a Masters in Counselling Psychology. And even more unbelievable – in marriage and family counselling. Wow. How is this possible? So, as a step of blind faith and in general, a directional agreement, we moved to Chicago in the fall of 1979 to begin that program (Jody wasn't 2 years old yet).

It was there, during years six and seven, that God began to turn our marriage around...slowly but genuinely. We started trying at home at night in our little apartment, what I was learning in my grad classes on marriage during the day. These insights with application, commitment and a whole lot of Jesus, started to bring change. At least it did for us. I remember exactly where I was that day when I had clearly turned a corner in my heart toward Donalyn. It was in the basement of the seminary chapel by the cafeteria when I felt deep down inside again, that I wanted to go home to be with her. I loved her again. Hope and closeness were gaining momentum. A feel a big-time gratitude even to this day.

Upon graduation from grad school, I agreed to take a college teaching position at my alma mater, Briercrest Bible College. And you know it. My course-load included classes on Marriage & Family Issues, Ministry to Broken Homes, and Premarital Counselling. It was in that first year of teaching that I had watched the movie, Kramer vs Kramer.

So, in my mind, there's no doubt. You need premarital counselling. At least, I know we did.

And now to Jody – my amazing daughter. She is all grown up and has a great husband and beautiful family of her own. Though she would have little to no memory of our earlier struggle years, there is no doubt that our kids would have seen a real marriage with ongoing real issues to work through while they were growing up. Jody, though always teaching and speaking on God's plan for relationships mostly to junior high and high school students, her interest in building great marriages summited in her grad school program. There, she focused her Master's Degree on developing premarital education for this very age group – 13–19-year-olds. She is helping students every week in getting a healthier relational perspective for their future marriages.

From what we have seen and what Chris and Jody have told us, they haven't faced near the marital challenges we did. I am confident it is because of the unbelievably great premarital counselling they received! Well, you judge. It was from Donalyn and me. I know, crazy again. Imagine doing the marital sexuality talk with your daughter and future son-in-law! I shake my head...

What This Means for You

Jody and I, as a father-daughter team, are committed. If we have our way, you won't ever go through the kind of marital pain Donalyn and I did or ever put your kids through what young Billy Kramer faced when his parents split up. You are going to build strong to last long. You won't ever need to entertain separation.

It starts with Keeping Calm and Carrying On (referring to chapter 1). We have good news about marriage. We have a plan. And if you work the plan in this guidebook, you'll get something great.

Don't fool yourself. Neither of you are perfect. You both have work to do. So, let's get to it.

The Ideal "I Do" series is two books. Book 1: Building Strong for pre-marriage. Book 2: Lasting Long for new marriage. Here are the 4 ways to get the most out of this premarital or new marriage series.

Be Committed – To work now on your relationship, talking through a host of issues, is an amazing foundation for your marriage. Be engaged. Do the work. Don't be lame. A half-hearted preparation will yield to a half-hearted marriage. Be a keener. Marriage is one test in life that you want to pass with 'flying colors.' Work hard and finish strong.

Be Honest – This may be somewhat scary but transparency is key to building a foundation of trust. It is better to work through any 'disclosure' challenges now than to face 'discovery' challenges later. Don't ask yourself, "I wonder if I should share this." Determine to share your junk now. Even the hard things – the embarrassing things. Allow them to love you for who you are - knowing even the challenging stuff about you.

Be Excited – Marriage is such a good thing! Beyond the gift of God's grace in my life, Donalyn and our ongoing marriage, is by far the greatest gift I have been able to enjoy and cultivate in my life. At the time of writing, we are 49 years marriage and Jody & Chris are 22 years in. You see, finding a great spouse is an incredible gift from the Lord – it's His favour on you.

Be Surrendered – Jody and I, along with our spouses, would all maintain that making Jesus Lord of your life and putting Him in the center of your marriage is the best way to succeed in life. My life statement is – *Put God First – Life Goes Best*! We believe it. Whether you are there yet in your faith or not, join us in this great journey of discovery toward a fabulous marriage – The Ideal "I Do" – pursuing the marriage you'll love.

Chapter 1
Keep Calm and Carry On:
The Good News About Marriage
Dr. Dave Currie

Winston Churchill's tenacious spirit was undoubtedly what inspired the British government to produce this famous morale-boosting poster from World War II *"Keep Calm and Carry On"*. It has now been re-used for all sorts of purposes – Keep calm & get along – Keep calm & keep fishing – Keep calm & drink wine – Keep calm & play ball, etc.!

The original Winston Church version – *"Keep Calm and Carry On"* – was created to steady the nation against the reoccurring, formidable and crushing attacks and pending invasion by enemy forces. Its hope-filled, courageous tone can still serve to anchor us against another daunting enemy – that of the very negative and unnerving statistics about the state of marriage today. Stay with me. You'll see there's reason to keep calm and carry on in your marriage as I seek to debunk a number of myths.

Let me start by setting the record straight. I am an honest man and I believe a genuine apology is in order. I am haunted by the fact that as a leader in the marriage and family field, I too have parroted that these two common notions were true. I have, like many others, repeated what I now am relieved to know to be false. I spoke publicly that:
- About 50% of marriages end in divorce
- The divorce rate within the church is the same as that in society at large

I know you've likely heard similar stats reiterated from other reliable sources as to the truth about where marriage is supposedly at in society and within the church. Very discouraging.

Well, I am sorry. We were wrong. I was wrong. How was that possible – me saying that?

But hang on – there is really GOOD NEWS coming.

I had mistakenly assumed the reliability of these marriage statistics that 50% of marriage ended in divorce. In response, I determined to boldly challenge couples in my sphere of influence to take the covenant of marriage seriously, warning of the very slippery slope into failure. My goal was to give the tools and tips needed to get every couple I could inspire onto the winning half of successful marriages. I know, what was noble in intention was still very discouraging. Can you see with me how I had left people with the depressing impression that their marriage had only a 50-50 chance of making it?

There's more. I began operating with the understanding that Christian marriages failed at the same rate as those outside the church. After all, don't we all trust Barna Research (The highly-trusted Christian polling firm)? I would speak of this sad truth as the topic would arise, and I am guilty of perpetuating a very negative myth. I would strongly express the need for people to live out that faith in the four walls of their home. The challenge, though well intentioned, left people wondering that if this stat was true, then what difference does God really make in a life, a marriage and a home.

In my heart, I wondered the same. This stat was disheartening, but with determination, I would rally undaunted around the faith and marriage flag. Yet in my gut, it didn't make sense. I didn't see anywhere near a 50% carnage rate in marriages in the faith circles I was in. This high divorce rate in the church didn't make sense to me. I reasoned it must be really bad elsewhere. I repeatedly surmised that while the divorce rate in our culture was high, it still didn't jive from my faith perspective that God in a marriage really changes things. I felt that knowing God really did make a great difference.

The Good News is that He does.

What I will share here is heavily dependent on Shaunti Feldhahn's fabulous research revealed in her book, *The Good News About Marriage: Debunking Discouraging Myths About Marriage and Divorce.* It is the only book in over twenty years that I have read twice (other than my Bible, of course). Space won't allow me to give all the justification behind Feldhahn's well-researched conclusions, but for those interested, you can get the book and read the brilliant documentation and encouraging details for yourself.

Understand the Good News About Marriage

TRUTH 1: The actual divorce rate has never been close to 50 percent! Instead of one in two marriages ending in divorce, it's closer to one in five. The average first marriage divorce rate across the general population is around 20%. If you take in all marriages, (second, third and more) the divorce rate is still only around 33 - 35%. So, if you are tracking with me, it means that couples getting married today have an 80% chance of having a lasting and satisfying marriage! Feldhahn says, "Imagine the difference in our collective unconscious if we say 'most marriages last a lifetime' rather than 'half of marriages end in divorce.'"

Where did the myth of a 50% divorce rate originate? When 'no fault' divorce was passed and made into law, there came with it a huge increase for a few years in the number of divorces as countless couples ran to the courts to more easily end unhappy unions. With this growing increase through the 1970-80 decade came the **PROJECTION** that if the trend continued, we'd soon see a 50% divorce rate. It was **PROJECTION,** only not the actual statistic. Sadly, this projected 50% divorce rate took on a life of its own. It went from being a point of conjecture to a widespread assumption to a perceived fact. The divorce rate has never ever hit 50% – try 35% during its all-time worst year (1980).

TRUTH 2: The divorce rate is declining and has been for over thirty-five years. The failure rate in marriage peaked in 1980 following the decade of the "no fault divorce" laws sweeping across almost all the states and later into Canada (The first state was California in 1970 with all but two states following suit by 1983. In Canada, no fault divorce came in 1986). Through this new marriage law, divorce became so easy.

TRUTH 3: Most married people today (88%) enjoy being married to their spouse and, given the chance, would do it all over again. Not only do most marriages make it, they do more than survive. They thrive and describe themselves as happy in their relationship. Feldhahn's research further shows that most of those couples that aren't happy would be if they stayed committed during hard times for five years.

TRUTH 4: Active faith clearly lowers the divorce rate almost in half. Again, Feldhahn's research shows that every study ever conducted on faith's impact on marriage has found that weekly church attendance alone lowers the divorce rate by between 25 and 50%, depending on the study. Couples who live their faith together and practice it through regular reinforcement within a church community generally have strong and lasting marriages. Thus, research does reveal that having a real and engaged faith does impact your marriage in a fabulous way with a divorce rate as low as 10-15 %.

The myth of the divorce rate being as high within the church as outside it originated with a 2001 Barna study that showed that professing Christians had a same divorce rate as non-professing Christians. The researchers were studying those who ***professed*** to hold Christian beliefs not those who went to church. They analyzed what people said they believed and its relation to marriage. What people say they believe but don't practice wasn't taken into account. There are a lot of people in the general population (especially in the US) who say they believe the Biblical truths but it doesn't affect their life. The gap of misunderstanding in the study was the difference between belief and practice. Those who attend church regularly and have the same faith commitment as their spouse have an incredibly higher success rate in marriage. The divorce rate is NOT the same in the church as outside it – it's half as much.

Embrace the Good News About Marriage

Donalyn and I got married young. In the 1970s, this was much more common than it is today. The odds aren't good for teen marriages then or now (we were nineteen). But my mother made a comment to me that I have never forgotten. She said, "Dave, I know you and Donalyn are getting married young, but you will make it because you have the LORD." I hung onto those words when we had seasons of marital difficulty. I truly believed and sought to live out that God does make a difference in a life, a marriage and a home. An active faith is a transforming faith – marriage included. Knowing and following God's plan radically does make a difference.

So where should we go from here? Here are three suggestions:

1. **Appreciate the good news**. Let the truth sink in. The divorce rate is not – I repeat NOT – at 50%. For first marriages, you have an 80% chance of being with your spouse for life. Further, God does make a difference in your marriage if and when you practice your faith together with the divorce rate within the church being as low at 10-15%.

2. **Advertise the good news.** Tell someone. Refer to this chapter in your discussions with friends, work associates and neighbors. Talk about it within your family. Pass it on to the leaders in your church. Help debunk the negative myths that too many are holding on as true.

3. **Adjust to the good news.** Rest in knowing that YOUR new marriage can make it even when you may go through a tough season. Don't live another day under the misunderstanding that when facing tough times you are on the verge of divorce. Garbage. Stay committed. Work through your issues. I have yet to see a marriage fall apart where both husband and wife have soft hearts toward God and His plan for their life and marriage.

Finally, young Christian couples – **keep calm and carry on!** Following the Lord does make a huge difference on both the satisfaction and longevity of your most important relationship. That's the really good news about marriage!

DISCUSSION STARTERS:

1. What discouraging news had you heard over the years about the lack of success in marriages. Where do you recall first hearing it? Who or what was the source?

2. The divorce rate is declining. Your marriage has as a minimum an 80% chance of success. If you are a Christian couple, you have a 90% chance of having a long and satisfying marriage. What do these truths do to your perspective and attitude toward your marriage? Share three thoughts:

   -
   -
   -

3. What or who do you think gives you your greatest boost that will help you to keep working at your marriage when the going gets tougher?

Chapter 2
Mastering Commitment:
The Whole You and Best Me
Jody Wandzura

Everyone starts in marriage saying they will have the Ideal *"I do!"* They anticipate that they will be together forever. They have heard the odds against being happily married, but they are sure their love will see them through any difficulty. Their love is stronger and deeper. They will be the ones who defy the odds because they are truly "in love!"

On the wedding day, couples recite vows to each other. The message is usually the same, whether we write them or say the traditional vows. We promise to stay committed – no matter what! "For better or worse, for richer or poorer, in sickness or health, to love and to cherish, til death do us part."

Chris and I wrote our vows and read them to each other at our wedding. I wanted to make sure we would remember our promises, so I had them engraved on two plaques for our first Christmas and hung them on either side of our wedding picture. They are now framed in our hallway, and on each anniversary, we read them to each other. We are both committed to keeping our vows for life.

Commitment is about being faithful, having eyes only for one and being exclusive to that one for a lifetime. It is much more than "I will remain in the same house as you no matter how much we dislike each other!" There is also the part that promises to love and cherish – a considerable step beyond being committed and staying in the marriage.

When you sign up for marriage, what are you pledging to? Isn't marriage supposed to be just like dating but with a new level of responsibility? When you get married, you promise to be faithful forever, but you must recognize that no one is perfect and you can't change others. Therefore, you must practice two kinds of commitment: The Best ME and the Whole YOU.

The Best ME Commitment

As humans, we are sinful and in a pre-perfect state. We need to take out the magnifying glass to our *OWN* lives and ask the Holy Spirit to show us areas where we need to grow. When I asked God to show me places where I needed to change, there were lots!

This first part of commitment requires awareness, humility, and hard work when reflecting on myself. It says, "I am in this relationship with my whole heart, and I am willing to change *anything* to be the best spouse I can be." Sometimes, it is challenging to see the blind spots in our own lives.

Therefore, an effective way to become your best version of you is to find a mentor or an accountability person. A mentor is someone who is ahead of you in age or experience. You could ask them questions and glean wisdom from them. An accountability person is more of a peer you openly share everything with, who asks you the tough questions and challenges you on how you are living your life. Regardless of our choice, we are wise to schedule regular discussions with them to be most effective.

Another way to become the best version of yourself is to find people in your life who have wonderful character and try to spend more time around them.

- My sister-in-law never holds a grudge and forgives freely; I always want to be a more gracious person when I am around her.
- I had a basketball teammate who always responded calmly in conflict; I learned that a gentle answer turns away wrath.
- My co-worker wholeheartedly trusts God and lives "with her hands wide open." I have learned generosity from her.
- My mom is the kindest and most fun-loving person I know; I like what she brings out in me.
- My husband is quick to serve others. It makes me want to do the same.

These are a few people who have inspired me to be the best me!

The Whole YOU Commitment

This second truth is about grace, patience and understanding for the other person. One recognizes that everyone comes as a full package – strengths and weaknesses. When you choose someone in marriage, you love and admire their strengths but are pretty aware of their weaknesses. These character deficiencies or annoying habits will not disappear because you walk down the aisle. They might even become more bothersome as time goes on.

We can easily see each other's faults in a close relationship like marriage. If you take out the magnifying glass on your spouse, you will detect many defects. If so, should you be the first to point out all of your partner's faults? No. Not helpful. Put the magnifying glass away. Instead, you need to trust that they are working on themselves (the Best Me Commitment) and pray that God gives them the strength and insight to make the necessary changes.

Before I met my husband, I dated other guys who were nice people, but each of them had more flaws or baggage than I cared to deal with for the rest of my life. When I met my husband to-be, I was amazed by his character, story of forgiveness, kindness to everyone and easy-to-get-along-with personality. I liked how practical and financially-wise he was. He was a quieter person, and he told me that he enjoyed listening! Most of all, I was drawn to his intention of obeying God. When I met him, his motto was TNC, which stood for "Today, No Compromise!" Wow! What a guy! He seemed *perfect*!

Over the years, I noticed he wasn't quite as perfect as I thought. His quiet side rarely shared more than "good" about his day. His financially-wise side stopped buying me flowers, and I almost died when he told me he didn't value gifts! His TNC motto ended many of our movie nights. I was feeling a little frustrated.

Finally, I gave my head a shake! These areas were more like 1% imperfections compared to the 99% amazing character. When I said "for sure" (actual words I said at the proposal) to marry Chris, I accepted him as he was. I needed to decide that even though he wasn't perfect, *he was perfect for me.* I now know that I am the most blessed woman in the world!

The Whole YOU Commitment requires us to receive our spouse as a complete package. We acknowledge their strengths and weaknesses and recognize that it is not our job to point out their flaws, nor should we try to change them. Instead, we pray that God will give us soft hearts toward change and mold our character to be the best spouse we can be (Phil 1:6). The Best ME and the Whole YOU – let's keep our vows for life.

DISCUSSION STARTERS:

1. Did you write your wedding vows? What did you promise to do? If you haven't written them, discuss what is important to you. What commitments do you want to make?

2. The Best Me Commitment says, "I am not perfect. God, what areas could I change in my life?" (Go ahead, say it now.) What did God bring to your mind?

3. The Whole You Commitment says, "No one is perfect, so I don't expect YOU to be perfect either." (Actually, stop and communicate this to each other right now.)

4. Discuss how you each have strengths and weaknesses. Name two of your partner's strengths and why you love them. Then, list one personal area of your weakness and how you might address it.

5. Talk about a person you admire for a particular character trait and explain how you would like to be more like that.

What God Says About Commitment:

1. **True marital love is shown by our life-long commitment to our spouse. We choose to honor God, His institution of marriage and your spouse by being faithful in every way until we part in death.**

   Proverbs 3:3-4 – *Let love and faithfulness never leave you*; bind them around your neck, write them on the tablet of your heart. Then you will win favor and a good name in the sight of God and man.

   1 Corinthians 13: 7 – If you love someone, you will be *loyal to him no matter what the cost.* You will always believe in him, always expect the best of him, and always stand your ground in defending him. TLB

   Song of Solomon 8:6-7 – Place me like a seal over your heart, like a seal on your arm; for love is as strong as death, its jealousy unyielding as the grave. It burns like blazing fire, like a mighty flame. *Many waters cannot quench love*; rivers cannot sweep it away. If one were to give all the wealth of one's house for love, it would be utterly scorned.

2. **Our vows matter to God. They are a covenant between us and our spouse – a bond of trust. We choose to fulfill our life promise – keep our word that we gave to our spouse in the presence of God, family and friends even when it's not easy.**

   Ecclesiastes 5:4,5 – When you make a vow to God, *do not delay to fulfill it*. He has no pleasure in fools; *fulfill your vow*. It is better not to make a vow than to make one and not fulfill it.

   Psalm 61:5 – For you, God, *have heard my vows*; you have given me the heritage of those who fear your name.

   Psalm 116:14 – I will *fulfill my vows* to the Lord in the presence of all his people.

   Psalm 89:34 – I will *not violate my covenant* or alter what my lips have uttered.

   Deuteronomy 23:23 – *Whatever your lips utter you must be sure to do*, because you made your vow freely to the LORD your God with your own mouth.

   Proverbs 2:16-17 – Wisdom will save you also from the adulterous woman, from the wayward woman with her seductive words, who has left the partner of her youth and *ignored the covenant she made before God*.

3. **Marriage is designed by God to be for life. Divorce is simply not His plan – as a matter of fact, God hates divorce – it is not an option for the Christian couple. God wants us to work out our issues – to always reconcile. God's target for marriage is that it lasts for life.**

   Mal. 2:13-16 – Another thing you do: You flood the LORD's altar with tears. You weep and wail because he no longer looks with favor on your offerings or accepts them with pleasure from your hands. You ask, "Why?" It is because the LORD is the witness between you and the wife of your youth. ***You have been unfaithful to her, though she is your partner, the wife of your marriage covenant.*** Has not the one God made you? You belong to him in body and spirit. And what does the one God seek? Godly offspring. So be on your guard, and ***do not be unfaithful to the wife of your youth***. "The man who hates and divorces his wife," says the LORD, the God of Israel, "does violence to the one he should protect," says the LORD Almighty. So be on your guard, and ***do not be unfaithful***.

   Matt. 19:3-8 – Some Pharisees came to him to test him. They asked, "Is it lawful for a man to divorce his wife for any and every reason?" "Haven't you read," he replied, "that at the beginning the Creator 'made them male and female,' and said, 'For this reason a man will leave his father and mother and be united to his wife, and the two will become one flesh'? So they are no longer two, but one flesh. ***Therefore what God has joined together, let no one separate."*** "Why then," they asked, "did Moses command that a man give his wife a certificate of divorce and send her away?" Jesus replied, "Moses permitted you to divorce your wives ***because your hearts were hard***. But it was not this way from the beginning."

4. **Sexual purity is fully implied in marital faithfulness. God requires us to remain exclusive to one person in your affections and your sexuality. These principles are anchored in the 10 Commandments, not the 10 Suggestions.**

   Exodus 20:14, 17 – ***You must not commit adultery***. You must not covet your neighbor's house. ***You must not covet your neighbor's wife***, male or female servant, ox or donkey, or anything else that belongs to your neighbor."

   Hebrews 13:4 – Marriage should be honored by all, and ***the marriage bed kept pure***, for God will judge the adulterer and all the sexually immoral.

   Job. 31:1 – "I made a covenant with my eyes ***not to look lustfully at a young woman***."

   Eph. 5:3,5 – But among you there must ***not be even a hint of sexual immorality***, or of any kind of impurity, or of greed, because these are improper for God's holy people. For of this you can be sure: No immoral, impure or greedy person—such a person is an idolater—has any inheritance in the kingdom of Christ and of God.

Chapter 3
Understanding the Laws of Relational Equilibrium

Dr. Dave Currie

One fond childhood memory surrounds the pleasure of mastering the teeter-totter. In some areas, they are now banned. It's the playground apparatus that involves two children rocking up and down where they can push with their feet to go faster and higher. To fully enjoy the activity, you needed a friend near your size – an equal who could offset your weight. You needed balance.

Here's what I found. The bigger I was, the more I had to move toward my friend to make the ride work. To share the experience, the heavier one had to compensate for the lighter. They had to move toward the middle. I learned I could control others if I outweighed them. Similarly, I could be stranded in the heavens with a friend who out-weighed me. Finally, the farther I leaned away from my friend, the more I could control their experience.

A teeter-totter ride resembles many relationships – lots of ups and downs – and that's not always negative. But the bigger personality we have (aggressive, opinionated and confident), the more we have the tendency to dominate our spouse. To compensate for this self-servingness, we have to move toward our partner to keep balance. The heavier person emotionally can often control the discussion and the direction of the relationship. We have to move toward each other in marriage, to really work to listen and validate our partner, especially if we are the more forceful one. This intentionality works to even out the balance in the interaction.

This balance in the friendship is called **Relational Equilibrium**.

To create stability and satisfaction in marriage, we have to practice this balance. I have observed three basic laws that make a pleasurable interpersonal experience possible. Apply these truths and we are on our way to overcoming all inevitable the ups and downs life can bring to our marriage.

Law 1: Shared Purpose

The first law of relational equilibrium is *shared purpose*. This means that both husband and wife have a deep commitment toward building a great marriage. Their common goal is to do

13

whatever it takes to have a rewarding relationship they want to be a part of. Some couples actually talk through and write out a couple mission statement. You can see our version in the side box for an idea of what I am referring to. We waited far too long to write this out and be on the same page. You can do better.

This level of intentionality anchors the couple through any difficult times. It sure has us. Divorce is simply not an option – but neither is a lousy marriage. There is a determination for better communication, solving real issues and building a lasting, satisfying friendship. Good marriages honor God.

He wants our marriage to be priority to all the competing options of our day. We need to commit to meet our spouse's needs – to please them. Notice what is stated in 1 Corinthians 7:33-34:

"...a married man is concerned about the affairs of this world—how he can please his wife – and his interests are divided...a married woman is concerned about the affairs of this world—how she can please her husband."

COUPLE MISSION STATEMENT
Dave and Donalyn Currie
Revised June 1, 2000

With a full surrender to Jesus Christ and the difference He makes in both a life and a home, our marriage is a life-long adventure of committed and genuine friendship that:

1. Focuses on keeping our individual faith alive and growing

2. Rises above the routines of life and the pressures of tough times

3. Bonds with the crazy glue of laughter, openness, and passion

4. Displays persistent support and an exclusive faithfulness to the core

5. Models the realities of a healthy marriage up close and personal to our kids

6. Builds a home where people are strangely and supernaturally encouraged

7. Reaches our in love and service to family, friends and community

---

Remember, our marriages matter to God. He wants our faith to be lived out in the four walls of our home first. Commit to the shared purpose of a kicking-awesome marriage!

Law 2: Equal Voice

The second law of relational equilibrium is *equal voice.* Each spouse has the right to be heard. Both opinions matter. Now, opposites naturally do attract complementing each other's personalities, temperaments and gifting. Though this is a good thing overall, one person is often stronger when it comes to couple interaction. If not careful, the more forceful spouse can dominate the conversation and control the direction of the relationship. The other spouse sometimes loses their voice.

Marriage is the merger of two lives, not the canceling of one!

Is your relationship really a safe one? An equal one? Do each of you have the freedom to share how you feel without fear of reprisal or rejection? Are each of your opinions equally validated and integrated into your marital direction? Or is one of you calling all the shots?

This one-sided selfish tendency in marriage needs to stop. No topic should remain off limits; each should have the right to speak and give input into family decisions. Philippians 2:1-4 puts it as clear as you want to hear it:

"Do nothing out of selfish ambition or vain conceit. Rather, in humility value others (especially your spouse) above yourselves, not looking to your own interests but each of you to the interests of the others."

Marriage is two becoming one – two speaking as one voice – two selflessly blending their lives. It is not the canceling of one voice but the combining of two.

Law 3: Mutual Respect

The third law of relational equilibrium is *mutual respect*. It's how we treat our spouse. There is no excuse for bad behavior toward our partner. "You can't just say you love people; you must really love them and show it by your actions" (1 John 3:18). Give your mate your best behavior not your worst! We are supposed to treat our spouse with gentleness and respect or God will not hear our prayers (1 Peter 3:7). Tough words.

There needs to be a deep commitment that we will treat each other well regardless of the level of frustration. There is no room for harshness, impatience or disdain. Respectful, considerate treatment within the relationship is maintained regardless of how difficult a disagreement may be. The goal of mutual respect is to keep showing patience, kindness, gentleness and the other good fruit from God's spirit.

We can see how to maintain this closeness in Colossians 3:12-14:

> "Therefore, as God's chosen people, holy and dearly loved, clothe yourselves with compassion, kindness, humility, gentleness and patience (toward your spouse). Bear with each other and forgive one another if any of you has a grievance against someone. Forgive as the Lord forgave you. And over all these virtues put on love, which binds them all together (your spouse and your whole family) in perfect unity."

> **FAMILY MISSION STATEMENT**
> Chris & Jody Wandzura
> December 2006
>
> In our everyday lives we want to demonstrate to people the amazing difference Jesus makes in a family.
>
> To proclaim the Good News via the vehicle of the family - Love Jesus, love People, love Life.

Applying the Laws of Relational Equilibrium will give you a chance to experience a God-honoring balance in life's most important relationships.
- **Shared Purpose**
- **Equal Voice**
- **Mutual Respect**

Discuss these with your mate. If needed, take steps to move toward your spouse today. Start today toward Doing Family Right...God's way.

DISCUSSION STARTERS:

1. Where do you feel your relationship is most out of balance?

2. Where do you feel you have not been heard by your spouse? Share two examples.
    -
    -

3. Write out two things you personally could do differently to increase the presence of each of these principles.

    - **Shared Purpose**
        -
        -

    - **Equal Voice**
        -
        -

    - **Mutual Respect**
        -
        -

Chapter 4
Are You Fun to Live With?

Dr. Dave Currie

Are You Fun to Live With? That's a rather gutsy question to ask yourself. If we are not sure how we'd answer or what the truth might be, we can always ask those we live with. I dare you. Whether our spouse, kids, parents, siblings or a roommate, their responses could be enlightening and may cause some complicated but needed soul searching.

Most of us know how to put on a show for others. We put our best foot forward and project a positive demeanor as part of our public persona. We give the world our good side. But what about those we live with? I know. That's often another story. They get to see the real you – and the real me – complete with our 'dark side'.

By the way, the title of this chapter ***Are You Fun to Live With?*** is taken from the book by the same name by Lionel Whiston written in 1968. The only reason that I know about this book, though I have never read it, is because its title haunted my wife (her words, not mine) for years – at least until she addressed a few things in her own life. Here's why.

When Donalyn originally saw this little hardcover on the shelf in a bookstore, we were living those crazy busy and thankless years of parenting four preteens. I know she felt like some weird human mutation trying to be a taxi driver, drill sergeant, a referee and a mess-hall cook all in one body! She would say the title haunted her because she felt she'd have to say "no" to the question that she was not a fun person to live with. That's scary to me. If this kind, servant-hearted wife of mine felt this way, you know how her brash and outspoken Scottish husband would have to answer the question!

But I digress. Enough about us. ***Are YOU a fun person to live with?***

At our ***Fusion 2:1*** Marriage Event, which we have presented to over 7300 people, (Why not invite us to your church?) we actually spend quality time on this question in our Attraction talk. We maintain that, as a couple, ***"if you stop having fun, commitment alone won't keep your love alive."*** We try to coach couples on how to keep the attraction growing over the years.

That's where our laws of attraction come in – which, by the way, will help you to be a fun person to live with! They are built on the powerful relational equation as we see it...

Love = Commitment + Attraction

Law 1: You can't build a great marriage on commitment or attraction alone.

Both are needed. Commitment is the pledge to remain engaged and the promise of exclusiveness. Commitment keeps you faithful and working on the relationship even in the tough seasons of marriage. There are times when commitment holds us together.

Attraction is that magnetic charm that draws us to our spouse. It is true that the appeal is present when the marriage is at its best and yes, during the dating and honeymoon phases. But it's more. This pull is not a shallow thing but a critical thing by our definition. It involves healthy traits, attitudes, dispositions and actions that draw us to one another. It is a necessary component of the relationship and not a bonus. There are times when attraction holds us together.

Law 2: Commitment brings security – attraction brings enjoyment.

A genuine commitment allows our spouse to know that we are not going anywhere. Our vows are just that! They express a sincere pledge that we'll keep working on the relationship as a priority. This commitment will make us feel safe and secure in our marriage.

A growing attraction is our joint agreement to keep having fun together as well as to keep being fun to be around. It's like that fresh life-giving smell in the air after a much-needed rain. We can just feel things starting to come alive. This attraction brings a smile to our face and a peace in our heart and we just want to have more of it.

Law 3: Commitment and attraction both require a consistent and intentional effort.

What happens if we start coasting the day we get married? Answer: our relationship will gradually come to a stop. We need to keep taking turns pushing each other like two kids with a homemade go-cart.

Sociological research of the family shows this for on average, the powerful initial infatuation stage between two people newly married – that honeymoon feeling – lasts only 18 months. Eighteen MONTHS??? What then? Face it. Being faithful and being fun both will take work!

So, even as commitment is a choice; attraction too is a choice. We must be intentional. Even though it feels so easy at first when we are connecting, laughing and having fun, it's not always like that. It doesn't always come naturally. Speed bumps can become mountain ranges that can lead to years of rough road where we end up miles apart. UNLESS....

Unless you grasp the fact that for attraction to survive, it can no longer be by accident. We need to commit to being an attractive spouse. So, I ask, *Are you fun to live with?* We have the power to choose. 1 John 3:18 (NLT) says it well: "Let's not merely say we that we love each other [our spouse]; let us show the truth by our actions" – our genuine effort at being attractive.

Law 4: Factors of attraction are both innate and developed.

It's true; there have always been some definite traits that drew me to Donalyn. Her inborn kindness and friendliness flow out of her as naturally as water from a hose. She doesn't have to turn it on. It's part of who she is and who she will always be. That's why some traits are called 'innate' – they are part of our God-given personal style.

But we all have a 'dark side'. I've always admitted that if you could cut me open relationally, I'd bleed three characteristics: critical, judgmental and impatient. I totally need God to change me or at least soften me to a level of being tolerable. I need to work at being fun to be around or else my intensity will cause the people closest to me to stop coming around.

You see, if we find ourself being a stick in the mud, a grouch or just plain grumpy – we have to make changes. We can learn a new way to interact. God wants us to be more fun [pleasant, encouraging & thoughtful] to be around. In Proverbs, it says, "A cheerful heart [being fun and friendly] is good medicine" (17:22). Our refreshing spirit will bring healing to people. It also says, "A cheerful heart [being fun and friendly] is a continual feast" (15:15). People will keep coming back for a second helping of our warm and inviting disposition.

Law 5: Initial attraction differs from lifetime attraction.

Ok, with initial attraction, it's like we start with a full tank of gas and for a long time, it feels like everything in the marriage is running smooth, like we're going downhill. That's the easiest part of our journey. But when things get tougher as we experience steep hills and miles between gas stations, we can start to run on fumes. It's dangerous, and we can actually be left feeling stranded.

We have to keep putting relational gas in the desirability tank. Attraction is both something we do and something we are – but mostly it's the willingness to keep making an effort to bring a smile to our spouse's face. Remember what you would do when you were dating to win your spouse's heart. Now, put in a similar push to keep their heart. Keep learning how your spouse spells attraction. And from our experience, it keeps evolving over time. So keep asking, "What do you need from me?" Then listen, learn it and live it.

Law 6: When attraction leaves, a vacancy appears.

The final law of attraction is more of a warning. What happens if we stop having fun together? What transpires when the attraction fades? In time, a vacancy appears. A vacancy is an 'unoccupied position or place'. We can't love if we are not there or not making an effort to love our spouse well. The result is an "empty space" for someone or something else to fill.

When the emotional connection is lost, a void grows – like a huge cavern of all our unfulfilled hopes, dreams and promises. This void makes many people vulnerable and if the commitment isn't strong enough, a serious violation of the marriage is too easily possible – the draw toward someone else – or worse, an affair. The space is filled but not with your spouse. I see it all the time.

Proverbs 20:6 reads: *"Many claim to have unfailing love, but a faithful person who can find?"* Unfailing love keeps the fun alive and the marital growth happening. It's not just being faithful not to leave but faithful to never quit making our relationship better. We build the attraction and protect the marriage by being a fun and caring person to be with. May God help us put more smiles on our spouse's face.

Are you a fun person to live with? I think I am. For fun, I tracked down a fifty-six-year-old copy of Whiston's book by that name for Donalyn's birthday...all the way from a used bookstore in Florida.

DISCUSSION STARTERS:

1. Are you a fun person to live with? How would you score yourself and your partner? Score out of 10 – 10/10 being fabulous! Discuss each other's answers.

His Scores	**Her Scores**
HER- /10	HER- /10
HIM- /10	HIM- /10

   Agree to have more fun together. Carve out the time to start dating again and then work harder to be a fun person to live with.

2. Ask yourself in what ways do you lose the fun factor. Do you become a grouch, a party-pooper or critical? What is YOUR negative attitudinal display? Why do you think you are responding this way?

3. What three things could you do to be a more fun person to live with?

   -
   -
   -

What God Says About Connection:

1. **Connection is built through living trustworthy. We will be faithful to your spouse's best interests. We will be loyal, dependable and reliable. We do what we say. Our partner will know we have their back.**

   Proverbs 18:24 – One who has **unreliable friends** (or spouse) soon comes to ruin, but there is a friend who sticks closer than a brother.

   1 Corinthians 13:7 – If you love someone, **you will be loyal to him no matter what the cost.** You will always believe in him, always expect the best of him, and **always stand your ground in defending him.** TLB

   Proverbs 20:6 – Many claim to have unfailing love, but a **faithful person who can find**?

2. **Connection is built on truth. There is no room for lying, minimizing or any form of half-truths. Honesty is the only policy for a stable, solid marriage. Our word is your bond.**

   Ephesians 4:15 – **Speak the truth in love.**

   Psalms 34:13 – Keep your tongue from evil and **your lips from telling lies**.

   Proverbs 30:8 – **Keep falsehood and lies far from me**.

   Job 27:3,4 – As long as I have life within me, the breath of God in my nostrils,[4] my lips will **not say anything wicked**, and my tongue **will not utter lies**.

   Colossians 3:9-10 – **Do not lie to each other**, since you have taken off your old self with its practices [10] and have put on the new self, which is being renewed in knowledge in the image of its Creator.

3. **Connection involves feeling safe with each other. We show patience, a listening ear and validate our spouse's thoughts. We walk softly and wisely, not in anger. Angry people push others away. Selfish anger is never of God.**

   Proverbs 22:24 – Do not make **friends** with (or marry) a **hot-tempered** person, **do not associate with one easily angered.**

   James 1:19-20 – My dear brothers and sisters, take note of this: Everyone should be quick to listen, **slow to speak and slow to become angry**, [20] because human anger does not produce the righteousness that God desires.

Colossians 3:8 – But now you must also **rid yourselves of all such things as these: anger, rage, malice, slander, and filthy language from your lips.**

Ephesians 4:26-27 – In your anger do not sin: Do not let the sun go down while you are **still angry,** and do not give the devil a foothold.

Ephesians 4:29-31 – **Do not let any unwholesome talk** come out of your mouths, but only what is **helpful for building others up** according to their needs, that it may benefit those who listen. [30] And do not grieve the Holy Spirit of God, with whom you were sealed for the day of redemption. [31] **Get rid of all bitterness, rage and anger,** brawling and slander, along with every form of malice.

4. **Connection is others-centered. We willingly put our spouse first. We go out of our way for them. Rather than being demanding and controlling, we regularly sacrifice for them – doing for them what we would want them to do for us. We treat them well.**

John 15:13 – Greater love has no one than this: **to lay down one's life for one's friends** (spouse).

Matthew 7:12 – Here is a simple, rule-of-thumb guide for behavior: **Ask yourself what you want people to do for you, then grab the initiative and do it for** *them*. MSG

Philippians 2:1-4 – If you've gotten anything at all out of following Christ, if his love has made any difference in your life, if being in a community of the Spirit means anything to you, if you have a heart, if you *care*— then do me a favor: Agree with each other, **love each other, be deep-spirited friends.** Don't push your way to the front; don't sweet-talk your way to the top. **Put yourself aside, and help others (spouse) get ahead.** Don't be obsessed with **getting your own advantage.** Forget yourselves long enough to **lend a helping hand.** MSG

5. **Connection is clearly built on kindness, warmth and encouragement. You see, if we know the Lord, we have to treat people right – especially our mate. Be gracious. Live in harmony accepting each other's differences as a bonus to embrace not a problem to address. Got it? Be kind to your mate more than anyone else in the world.**

Colossians 4:6 – **Let your conversation be gracious and attractive** so that you will have the **right response** for everyone (especially your spouse). NLT

Romans 15:5-7 – May God, who gives this patience and encouragement, help you **live in complete harmony with each other,** as is fitting for followers of Christ Jesus. Then all of you can join together with one voice, giving praise and glory to God, the Father of our Lord Jesus Christ. Therefore, **accept each other just as Christ has accepted** you so that God will be given glory. NLT

Ephesians 4:32 – **Be kind and compassionate to one another,** forgiving each other, just as in Christ God forgave you.

Proverbs 18:1-3 – An **unfriendly person pursues selfish ends** and against all sound judgment **starts quarrels**. Fools find no pleasure in understanding but **delight in airing their own opinions**. When wickedness comes, so does contempt, and with shame comes reproach.

Proverbs 17:22 – **A cheerful heart is good medicine.**

Proverbs 15:15 – **A cheerful heart is a continual feast.**

1 Thessalonians 5:11 – Therefore **encourage one another and build each other up**, just as in fact you are doing.

2 Corinthians 13:11 – Finally, brothers and sisters, rejoice! **Strive for full restoration, encourage one another, be of one mind, live in peace.** And the God of love and peace will be with you.

Chapter 5
Take the Express Way:
Be a Better Communicator
Jody Wandzura

In most relationships, one person talks more than the other. My husband and I joke around about this. When we arrive home, I immediately report all my day's events. I then follow it up with, "How was your day?" His usual response to my daily question is "good." Every day seems the same. I often inquire more by asking rapid-fire questions. "How did that meeting go? How was chapel? How was practice? Did anything go wrong? Did you get everything done?" Early in our marriage, I remember feeling frustrated that although I heard about his day, I had to work too hard to get those answers composed of one-word tidbits. It was somewhat exhausting, and I felt that something was lacking.

Expressing oneself in marriage is more than just talking; it means "volunteering you" without our spouse peppering or forcing you to participate. We share who we are, what we like or dislike, what we think, and how we feel as we go through life. We openly contribute about ourself to connect on a deeper level and build a reciprocal friendship. When both people voluntarily express themselves, this creates a healthy and meaningful sharing of life.

One rainy day in May, after my usual question of "How was your day," Chris informed me that he felt drained from a challenging encounter with someone at work. Immediately, he had my attention as it was much more than the typical "good." He looked discouraged; his tone was quiet, and his body language showed defeat. As he shared the situation, I felt his frustration. I understood how his day had impacted him. He revealed his heart, and I gained a deeper insight into my husband's worldview through that trying situation. Most of all, I felt for him and wanted to improve things. Expression creates the opportunity to build empathy for the hard stuff and excitement for the good things.

Expressing ourself is a skill that we can learn with practice. It is like peeling back one onion layer at a time. We choose how many layers we should carefully peel back as we get to know someone. Anyone is welcome to hear the details of our day, but maybe not the outcome of the conversation with our boss. Can we trust this person to share our heart openly? Do they care about us? Once fully committed to each other, we should be willing to share everything to reach greater intimacy freely.

One big problem for some people is that they never peel back more than the top "good" layer. In those early years of our marriage, when expression was not Chris' forte, I added a further question to follow his routine "good" answer: "What does 'good' look like, sound like, and feel like?" It sounds like something a teacher would ask a student, but if my goal is to get to know my husband, then it is appropriate. Overall, this question has allowed us to grow in our communication. Most days, Chris would respond, "My day was good...and what does "good" look, sound, and feel like? Well, in the morning..." It is more work for him, but I appreciate it so much! Excellent communication takes effort.

Does any of this sound familiar in your relationship? One person may come from a family that never talked about what their day looked, sounded or felt like. Or perhaps you have been hurt in the past and now have a difficult time opening up completely. If you have never known how to express yourself, here are some discussion starters that could help you not only peel back the layers but also move your daily report to a real story with genuine emotion and empathy! Try anchoring your interaction around the acronym TTWA - Topic, Thankful, Wish and Action.

TOPIC
First, you must introduce a topic such as your day's events, job, health, family, or relationship. The subject of your conversation comes as a question to start the dialogue. Usually, this is the inquirer who asks the question, "How was your day (or whatever topic)?" But if I wanted to volunteer, I could pose the opening line like, "Is now a good time for me to share about my day (or a different topic)?" Or "Would it be ok if I share with you how my meeting went today?"

THANKFUL
Then, you develop the topic by answering, "What are you thankful for?" Your response lets you share your thoughts and feelings regarding the selected topic's good things. It lets you choose what *you* believe is essential to share and allow the other person to *see what you value*. Being thankful brings a sense of peace and joy and starts the conversation off with a helpful tone.

For example, if asked about your day, it might sound like this: "I was happy to arrive at work early as there was not a lot of traffic. Someone had already made coffee, so I enjoyed a cup in the staffroom. I had two hours to get work done before my first meeting, which was good because I had over forty-five emails in my inbox. The meeting took a while and was a bit heated, but the problems didn't impact me, so I listened quietly. The rest of my day just flew by."

WISH
Then you transition to the question, "What do you wish would be different and why?" This allows for the full spectrum of emotion to emerge for what you are thinking and how you are feeling. Now is your chance to vent about what is challenging for you. You might continue your explanation by pinpointing that one complicated issue: "I had one Zoom meeting that did not go well. The client was not willing to budge on his side of the agreement. I might lose this client, which will look bad. I feel stuck, though, as the business will not allow me to give him what he wants, but they expect me to keep him as a client *and* meet my sales quota. It seems unfair and is very frustrating. I don't know what to do."

ACTION

The conclusion of "Am I going to do anything about it?" is critical. It lets the person know your plans and if you need anything from them. If all you require them to do is listen, you conclude your story by saying, "So what I have decided to do is..." And then you thank them for giving their time and ear to the matter. If the person sharing does not conclude with any action plan, it would be great to ask, "Is there anything you can do to improve things?" or "Is there anything I can do to help?"

Overall, having each person freely express themself adds to the friendship and brings joy in sharing your story, peace in knowing that they trust you and freedom to peel back the layers of your heart safely.

DISCUSSION STARTERS:

1. Who is more likely to fully express their day's look, sound, and feel? Who needs more prompting? What is it you need to really feel heard?

2. Think about the TTWA acronym: topic, thankful, wish, action. Do you volunteer yourself in each of the areas? Which area do you find the hardest to share on and what is one thing you could begin to do to improve?

3. Have each person take turns sharing about their day trying the TTWA format.

What God Says About Communication:

1. **Plan on being completely truthful in your interaction with your spouse. Lies of any kind must end! Twisting the story is wrong. Honesty is the only policy!**

   Colossians 3:9-10 – [In marriage,] *do not lie to each other*, since you have taken off your old self with its practices and have put on the new self, which is being renewed in knowledge in the image of its Creator.

   Ephesians 4:25 – Therefore, each of you must *put off falsehood and speak truthfully* to your [spouse], for we are all members of one [family].

   Proverbs 24:26 – [In marriage,] an *honest answer* is like a kiss on the lips.

2. **Look at life from your spouse's perspective. Put them first. Listen to their heart. Their opinion matters. Seek to understand what they are trying to say to you. Talk to them how you would like to be talked to.**

   Matthew 7:12 – So, in everything [in marriage,], *do to others what you would have them do to you*, for this sums up the Law and the Prophets.

   Philippians 2:3-4 – [In marriage,] do nothing out of *selfish* ambition or vain conceit. Rather, in *humility value others above yourselves*, not looking to your *own interests* but each of you to *the interests of the others*.

   Romans 12:10 – [In marriage,] *be devoted* to one another in love. *Honor one another above yourselves*.

3. **Treat your spouse well. Be gracious. If there were ever anyone who you should be kind, sensitive and patient with, it would be your mate. Make it happen.**

   Ephesians 4:2-3 – [In marriage,] be completely *humble and gentle; be patient, bearing with one another in love*. Make every effort to *keep the unity* of the Spirit through *the bond of peace*.

   Colossians 4:6 – [In marriage,] let your conversation be *always full of grace*, seasoned with salt, so that you may know *how to answer* everyone.

   Proverbs 16:24 – [In marriage,] *gracious words* are a honeycomb, sweet to the soul and healing to the bones.

Chapter 6
Learning to Gel:
Building Lifelong Friendship
Dr. Dave Currie

I grew up on *"Jell-O"*. It's that rather inexpensive gelatin dessert that comes in a variety of flavors and colors. Looking back, Jell-O served as a staple product in most poor families' cupboards. Add carrots and celery, and presto, it was a salad. Stir in marshmallows and top with whip cream and sprinkles and bingo...it's a dessert. Jell-O conforms to the shape of the container it is put into, sometimes even a mold like a Christmas tree or a heart. I distinctly recall my mother teaching me how to make Jell-O – pretty simple, even for a preschooler. Just add the powder to hot water, stir, chill and eat.

Jell-O is much like friendship in marriage – two radically different colors and flavors of people when mixed together and put in the right environment, can gel uniquely and become inseparable forever. Combined, they take on this new shape called a "couple," and the new blend of connection is something both desirable and delicious.

God talked about two becoming one in marriage in a way that no man should ever try to separate. Great idea, this two gelling into one (see Mark 10:8). It was God's plan for the marital commitment to be a lifelong friendship. My goal is to make a few suggestions to help you get the right mix in your marital mold – one that satisfies both of you. To build an ongoing and growing companionship with your spouse, there are five key ingredients you'd be wise to consistently stir in. In doing so, you'll more fully enjoy your mix.

Thrills
For friendship in marriage to grow, it is critical to keep doing things that get both of your blood pressures higher – and no, I am not talking sex! It's being intentional about just having plain old fun. That's the thrill part, and I think many of us grow up far too fast after we get married. You learned how to enjoy each other in your dating years doing all kinds of wild and crazy things. It didn't matter much what it was. I remember ice cream fights, surprise dates, and little trinket gifts we'd give that we found a way to give meaning to. I still enjoy impromptu races or meaningless competitions where one of us usually cheats to declare a win. There have been late night swims in cold lakes or getting dressed up to go to a fancy-shmancy restaurant. Our fun includes snorkeling, finding a favorite crepe place, roller-blading, sunset walks, mountain hikes, playing crib and a favorite park to swing together in. Keep the thrills coming – do things together. Be willing to pretty much go anywhere or do anything for the sole reason of seeing your spouse smile one more time.

Tenderness

Another key aspect of marital friendship is building a state of endearment between you. These are the signs that you are still 'in love'. At the heart of true love is selflessly thinking about the other when you are not even with them. It's keeping them on your mind by making calls, sending texts and emails merely to show ongoing interest in how their day is going. It comes out in an overall softness toward them. Kind treatment is essential, but is as simple as getting her a coffee when you're getting one or putting toothpaste on his toothbrush. It's living in true tandem where day-to-day happiness between you is the norm. This aspect of love displays you know them well enough to be sensitive to their needs – inside and out. Tenderness includes reassuring touch, supportive hugs and encouraging words that warm the heart. It knows when to just listen. So, hold hands in public. Hug often. Speak with gentleness and respect. Be patient. Let your spouse receive your best treatment.

Trust

Trust is a two-sided coin. It includes who you are when away from your spouse and with others, and also who you are when alone with just each other. On one side, it holds a deep assurance that "I know I am unique. I am your one and only. There are no close seconds." We live in a world of relational compromise. It is often trumpeted, "What happens in Vegas, stays in Vegas." Very foolish thinking. Yet, many spouses somehow seem to justify outside friendships with old flames, Facebook friends, and co-workers.

Simply put, you maintain trust between you by living trustworthy. Friendships with others of the opposite sex require healthy relational boundaries. To build trust when you are away from each other, a fierce loyalty must exist, a true faithfulness to the core. Your spouse needs to feel safe when NOT with you.

On the other side of the trust coin, your spouse has to feel equally safe when they are with you. Do you keep your word? Do you speak the truth? Can you keep a confidence? Are you open and honest?

There needs to be a sense of exclusiveness on the comments made to each other. When hearts are shared, the discussion won't go anywhere. You need to feel free to be "you" without scrutiny or belittling. You are never criticized in front of others. Difficult issues are always handled privately and respectfully. You work to forgive fully, freely and frequently. You feel each other's respect. You have a unique and safe place in each other's hearts. That's the two sides of the spirit of trust in lasting friendship.

Thankfulness

To live thankful is to validate your spouse's contributions in your life. Face it. We are drawn to grateful people. It is nice to be noticed for the part we play in life. To grow your friendship in this area includes showing appreciation for routine things your spouse does daily. Don't take each other for granted.

It's also remembering to express sincere gratitude for the extra special effort they make to help you – it's noticing when they go above and beyond to display their love to you. Show your pleasure and express your joy over the thrills shared, the tenderness shown and the trust expressed. Include in your forms of gratitude hugs of appreciation, notes of thanks, emails of acknowledgement and texts of admiration.

Extend appreciation for who they are from time to time and not just what they do for you. Be sure to put your heart into it; don't just say the words. Frankly, the greater the effort your spouse makes, the greater your expression of gratitude. Flaunt your approval for your spouse in front of others too. There's nothing like bragging about them to shout our appreciation. Your spouse won't get tired of you if you are consistently acknowledging and constantly appreciating their contributions. Be thankful for them.

Togetherness
This final aspect of companionship may be as much a result as an intention. It's about being deeply connected in heart and in life. God was right in the first place (we are not surprised) when He said that it was not good for man to be alone but He will make a partner suitable for him (Genesis 2:18). There is nothing like having a true counterpoint in another person – one who is your life compliment. Possibly the greatest joy to the human heart is to be known and still loved – by God for sure but also from at least one other person, usually your spouse.

You can't be known or get to know them in a vacuum. It takes time. Get into each other's schedules for chunks of time together. Always choose to carve out moments to connect daily. Share openly. Offer yourself. Work toward having the two of you to become one unit – distinct people appreciated for their unique perspective but also two that willingly lay down their independence to have real oneness.

Like two blades of a scissors that, once combined and working together, create something powerful and effective, combining your lives in lasting friendship is a great tool in the hands of God. Look forward to being together, playing together, laughing together, talking together, praying together and a host of other togethers. Make the effort to truly be 'one'.

Okay, so you admit your marriage may not be gelling like Jell-O. It is never an instant stir and mix. Many couples start missing this growing friendship. At different times in our over forty-nine years of marriage, our connection has been lacking too. Maybe you, like too many others, will only appear to have a good marriage. Work to engage. Don't live with a huge distance between you – being separated within the same house. If the fun is missing, words are sharp, trust has eroded and there is little to no connection, please don't quit now. We all go through tough times like this.

If you are wanting to have the right ingredients in your companionship, it's time to talk and really engage. Use this chapter to stir things up on how well you are doing. Make your marriage a priority. Ask God for help and his perspective on what you need to work on. Wise couples are willing to go to any length to fully understand and appreciate who their spouse is. They commit to work toward an awesome marriage. I hope things really start to gel between you.

DISCUSSION STARTERS:

1. Evaluate the five aspects of building a life-long friendship in your relationship so far. Rate out of 10 how you feel you are doing as a couple in each area:

   - THRILLS – having fun and laughter together   /10

   - TENDERNESS – treating each other very kindly   /10

   - TRUST – being safe when with them or apart   /10

   - THANKFULNESS – sharing appreciation to them often   /10

   - TOGETHERNESS – knowing a true oneness in all we do   /10

2. After recognizing which aspect of marriage you see yourselves weakest at, write down three things you would like to try to help you *'gel'* better in this area.

   Weakest Aspect: _____

   -

   -

   -

3. What is the most fun you ever had together? Describe the event.

4. What's the nicest thing your spouse has ever done for you?

5. What's the biggest surprise they ever pulled off for you?

What God Says About Companionship:

1. **God built us to be meaningfully related to someone. To love and be loved is one of the greatest gifts we enjoy. Pairing up with a suitable life partner is the norm for most people due to the deep need for companionship.**

   Genesis 2:18 – The LORD God said, "It is not good for the man *to be alone*. I will make a helper *suitable for him*."

   Proverbs 18:22 – He who finds a wife *finds what is good* and *receives favor* from the LORD.

   Ecclesiastes 4:9-12 – *Two are better than one*, because they have a good return for their labor: If either of them falls down, one can help the other up. But pity anyone who falls and has no one to help them up. Also, if two lie down together, they will keep warm. But how can one keep warm alone? Though one may be overpowered, two can defend themselves. *A cord of three strands is not quickly broken* (braid God in as the third strand).

2. **A great friendship requires putting your spouse's needs and interests before your own. Working to let go of our selfish nature is one of our first hurdles in marriage. Putting our mate first is hard.**

   Romans 12:9-10 – Love must be sincere. Hate what is evil; cling to what is good. [10] Be devoted to one another in love. *Honor one another above yourselves*.

   Phil. 2:3-4 – Do nothing out of selfish ambition or vain conceit. Rather, in humility *value others above yourselves*, [4] not looking to your own interests but each of you to the interests of the others.

   Romans 15:1,2 – We who are strong ought to bear with the failings of the weak and *not to please ourselves*. [2] Each of us should *please our neighbors* [our spouse] *for their good*, to build them up.

   1 Corinthians 7:33-34 – ...a married man is concerned about the affairs of this world—*how he can please his wife*— [34] and his interests are divided [and] a married woman is concerned about the affairs of this world—*how she can please her husband*.

3. **With real friendship, words are not enough. Talk is cheap. Love must show. A great marriage is seen in how well two treat each other.**

   1 John 3:18 – Dear children, let's not merely say that we love each other; *let us show the truth by our actions*. NLT

1 Peter 1:22 – "***Love one another deeply***, from the heart.

I Thess. 5:11 – Therefore ***encourage one another and build each other up***, just as in fact you are ***doing***.

1 Cor. 13:4-8 – ***Love is*** patient, love is kind. It does not envy, it does not boast, it is not proud. [5] It does not dishonor others, it is not self-seeking, it is not easily angered, it keeps no record of wrongs. [6] Love does not delight in evil but rejoices with the truth. [7] It always protects, always trusts, always hopes, always perseveres. Love never fails.

1 Peter 4:8 – Above all, ***love each other deeply***, because love covers over a multitude of sins.

Chapter 7
Woodpeckers and Turtles:
Do Opposites Attract or Attack?
Dr. Dave Currie

You've likely heard someone make reference to the celebrated book by Dr. John Gray, *Men are from Mars and Women are from Venus*. In it, Gray helps people to understand male–female differences. That is significant. We don't easily *understand* the opposite sex and how differently they think from us. But there is something more going on in the mate selection process than simply being attracted to the opposite sex. Understand what this is and you'll improve your marriage almost instantly!

People are also drawn to – powerfully attracted to – someone who has **personality differences** that compliment who they are. Understand that...

OPPOSITES ATTRACT

Research consistently shows that **opposites do attract**. Like a moth to a porch light, we are charmed by those who can fill in our gaps; who are our compliment. God knew what He was doing when He wired people to be enticed to their counterpoint. We call these alluring differences *personal style*. It is how a person looks at and approaches life.

This opposite attraction is a good thing. Our personal style differences combine to make us stronger as a couple than when alone. No one is redundant. It's like you complete each other. Relational equilibrium in a marriage can be achieved when opposite people come together and live to respect and value these uniquenesses – what drew them to you in the first place. Through the considerate merger of two very different people, we have a better chance to form balanced decisions and make sensible purchases. We are even more likely to raise well-adjusted kids who are a mix between a very different but complimentary mom and dad. Again, this is all part of God's plan.

OPPOSITES ATTACK

While we concur that opposites attract, have you ever, like me, found that opposites can also attack? For years I wondered why Donalyn and I could butt heads so easily and so often. When do our personal style differences become such a hurdle? You likely have experienced similar tensions in your relationship.

The truth is, you love and are attracted to your mate's uniqueness 'most' of the time. But remember, opposite means just that – **OPPOSITE** – differing views, conflicting perspectives, opposing opinions, contradictory approaches, and even clashing wills. That's where the rub begins and the stress can set in. Our personal styles of approaching life – clear dispositional differences between you and your partner – though attractive initially, can easily create marital havoc later unless better understood.

PERSONAL STYLES

Check out these examples of personal style differences to help grasp how opposites could both attract and attack. Note: these are not male-female differences. They are dispositional differences. At times, your partner's traits that were once a draw to you can become a drain on you. You will likely see some of each other's relational styles listed here:

Quiet	Outspoken
Confident	Hesitant
Withdrawing	Engaging
Courageous	Timid
Extroverted	Introverted
Talkative	Private
Sensitive	Brash
Carefree	Worried
Methodical	Random
Driven	Laid back
Peacemaking	Argumentative
People-oriented	Project-oriented

By reading this list, you start to get the feel. We can begin to see why opposite styles sometimes attack? Our way of approaching life makes sense to us and thus becomes the "right" way doing things. *As a result of our experience, mixed in with a little (or a lot of) selfishness, stubbornness and insecurity, we tend to want to conquer, control or compete with our spouse instead of trying to compliment, collaborate and commend each other.* Wow. Read that last statement again.

Understanding each other's personal styles is key to developing a harmonious marriage. Knowing who you are and how you approach life can shed real light on the dark side of how you interact. As I'm sure you've experienced, style differences show up so clearly when disagreements and conflicts arise between you.

The WOODPECKER-TURTLE Style Continuum

We have found over the years that personal styles simply put can reflect two ends of a continuum. To help couples better understand their mates, we have developed the personal style self-test called *"the woodpecker-turtle quiz"*. This two-critter continuum reveals how a person generally approaches life and relationships. It's the key to appreciating your partner's interaction style.

Understanding each other's styles will greatly enhance your ability to solve your disagreements in a healthier way. Remember, too, that the two extremes are not wrong, just different. And it is not a male-female thing either, like men are woodpeckers and women are turtles or vice versa. We have found a good balance of men and women at each end of the continuum.

Let's look closer at the two critters at the opposite ends of the personal style continuum.

The **TURTLE** – Here's a snapshot of the hard-shelled spouse. They are more passive and cautious, will mull things over, tend to withdraw, will avoid a fight, are more restrained, think first, are willing to let things go and often downplay the issues. They do "Turtle" to avoid conflict and tension and go into hiding!

The **WOODPECKER** – Here's the snapshot of the hard-nosed spouse. They are more aggressive and direct, are impatient, tend to press in, will start a fight, are more outspoken, speak first, don't let issues go and can magnify the issues. They do "peck" and create conflict by pestering and pursuing.

FACING THE DARK SIDE IN ALL OF US

It is wise to appreciate these personal style differences rather than discount them. Remember, there are good and bad things about being a turtle and good and bad things about being a woodpecker. Neither style is wrong or right.

The dark side of a turtle is how they use their hard shell to put up a wall. They turtle to protect themselves. This defensiveness causes them to withdraw emotionally and sometimes walk away physically. The stalling and stonewalling doesn't bring a solution but rather creates isolation and distance in the relationship. Turtles should agree to talk things out.

The dark side of the woodpecker is how they use their beak as a battering ram. They peck to get their point across. Their persistence in the discussion pushes their spouse away usually out of either fear or exasperation. Insistent woodpeckers will often follow their spouse around the home taking the discussion from room to room. Woodpeckers should agree to back off and solve things in stages.

It's time to understand yourself and your spouse better. Who's the woodpecker and who's the turtle? Take the quiz to begin your discussion on how you can better recognize your mate's personal style and then more effectively communicate and even avoid conflict in your marriage.

BOTH OF YOU TAKE THE QUIZ BELOW – Compare your answers! Discuss your differences.

The Woodpecker-Turtle Quiz

Dr. Dave Currie

INSTRUCTIONS: To determine your personal styles, for each statement, put a check below the spouse who, in your opinion, is more likely to say those words or whom the statement better represents. Tally the husband and wife totals with the guide below. Share your perspectives.

PERSONAL STYLE OF INTERACTION

		Wife	Husband
	Who is more likely to say:		
1.	It is easier to keep arguing than to let a discussion go.	___	___
2.	I often hold in my thoughts than speak them out.	___	___
3.	I tend to back off when I feel pressured or not heard.	___	___
4.	I am more likely to speak out than hold my thoughts in.	___	___
5.	It is easier to deny there is an issue than to really face it.	___	___
6.	I like to think through my words before speaking.	___	___
7.	I give up in exasperation when we are not getting anywhere.	___	___
8.	I often speak out my words before I think them through.	___	___
9.	I prefer to resolve things over time.	___	___
10.	I press on, committed to prove that I am right.	___	___
11.	It is easier to walk out than to keep arguing.	___	___
12.	I tend to pry to get my spouse to talk more about an issue.	___	___
13.	It is important to talk things through in spite of the tension.	___	___
14.	I realize that my silence and putting up walls may cause hurt.	___	___
15.	I am comfortable with conflict.	___	___
16.	I am often hesitant to share what I think.	___	___
17.	I am usually comfortable confronting my spouse.	___	___
18.	I prefer a context where I feel emotionally safe.	___	___
19.	I need to get things resolved as quickly as possible.	___	___
20.	I would rather let things go than escalate to a fight.	___	___
21.	I am generally uncomfortable with conflict.	___	___
22.	I get impatient when my spouse is holding back in discussions.	___	___
23.	I can second-guess what I am going to say.	___	___
24.	I realize that my criticism and harshness may cause hurt.	___	___
25.	I am okay with letting unresolved issues lie.	___	___
26.	I like to talk things through at my pace when I am good and ready.	___	___
27.	I willingly face issues head on.	___	___
28.	I prefer to avoid discussions that are uncomfortable for me.	___	___
29.	Unresolved issues between us bother me.	___	___
30.	I prefer conversations where we talk directly and honestly.	___	___

To identify your personal styles, circle the numbers below with a red pen for the wife and a blue for the husband.

W = 1, 4, 7, 8, 10, 12, 13, 15, 17, 19, 22, 24, 27, 29, 30 – Woodpecker is your style.

T = 2, 3, 5, 6, 9, 11, 14, 16, 18, 20, 21, 23, 25, 26, 28 – Turtle is your style.

Chapter 8
You Make No Sense:
Avoiding Marital Misunderstandings
Dr. Dave Currie

A man once called his neighbor to help him move a couch that had become stuck in the doorway. They pushed and pulled until they were exhausted, but the couch wouldn't budge. Fully exasperated, the man said as he threw up his hands, "Forget it; we'll never get this thing in."

The neighbor looked at him in confusion and said, "In?"

Do you ever feel like you and your spouse are working against each other? Misunderstandings kill connection. For some couples, it's this daily push and pull experience that robs them of joy in their marriage. Many bad habits perpetuate misunderstandings.

The Bible has a straightforward challenge for us, and let me aim it a little more at your home life. James 1:19 says, *"Understand this, my dear [married] brothers and sisters: You must all be quick to listen, slow to speak, and slow to get angry."* NLT

Listening and not getting defensive...that's not natural for me. Men, do you struggle sometimes, like me, understanding your spouse to the point that it feels like she's speaking a foreign language? Remember, we don't speak 'womanese'! Women, do you feel like you need a crowbar to get your guy to open up and really talk? If you, like us, feel at times that your partner makes no sense, why not consider trying some of these great suggestions to overcome your misunderstandings? This will be so critical as you move on in your marriage.

Learn to Listen
Sounds so easy. The longer you are married, the potentially harder listening can become. Why? Because I know my wife Donalyn so well, and have been through many similar discussions, I can tune her out almost automatically and simply press rewind on a previous discussion. That works only to a point but invariably creates a mess. All of us, men and women alike, have to learn to listen actively and patiently. Stop and face your spouse if possible. Not easy for us type "A's" who like to pace or are on the go! Get rid of all the distractions – like phones. Don't assume you know what our mate is going to say, and start formulating a response. You could miss their point entirely. Settle in, lean in and listen. Attempt to grasp what they are trying to say.

Listen Without Judgment
When you get the "here we go again" feeling inside, take a breath and decide to stop that inner downward spiral. Give them a clean slate, don't hold the past against them and listen without an edge. Give your mate the benefit of the doubt. Too often, I negatively read into my wife's

looks, her gestures, her facial expressions and her tone and assume the worst is coming. I start getting defensive. Then, I shut her out and don't really listen. I should know better.

Donalyn deserves to be heard, as does your mate. I need to fight the temptation to assume the worst and give her room to change if needed. The nature of my response often dictates the tone of the ongoing discussion. I must be quiet, stop and listen to her – and I don't just mean physical quietness, either. I need to refrain from rehearsing my argument. There are going to be times when harder things need to be said between you. Relax. Embrace the moment and learn all you can. It validates who your spouse is and respects how they feel. It fosters co-operation, rather than competition, between you.

Listen – Especially if You're the Talker
With most couples, there is one person who is more verbal. Two thirds of the time, it's the woman who shares easier, but sometimes it is the man who talks more (like me). It is especially important for the talker to learn good listening skills and to give their mate the time to talk. If you feel like your spouse isn't communicative enough, make sure you're giving them a chance to open up. If you are filling the air with your words, your spouse won't be able to share unless they fight for "air time". That isn't likely to happen, and it drives them deeper into privacy. Donalyn likes to think things through and is not instant in her responses. It used to frustrate me more than it does now. I try to give her the time she needs in our discussions. You don't have to ask her how often I am successful. I am still working on patience, okay?

Seek Clarification Over Frustration
How many times have you and your spouse had an argument, only to discover that the fight could have been avoided if you had truly taken the time to understand one another? My wife and I have had times where, as we worked through an area of disagreement, we discovered that we didn't really disagree at all – we only *thought* we disagreed because we were too impatient to fully understand one another. How dumb is that!

So many fights are escalated because we don't make the effort to clarify what the other person is trying to communicate. We say, "Well, I thought you said *this*…", and it wasn't *that* at all. It's important to clarify by saying, "If I hear you correctly, I hear you saying this…" Then, the other person says, "No, I didn't mean that, I meant this…" The spouse has a chance to restate him or herself, to ensure they are understood. Reacting without clarification leads to frustration! It's when your spouse doesn't make any sense to you. Take time to clarify.

Differing Opinions Aren't Wrong
Men and women are different…and that's okay. I have different opinions than the guys I play hockey with. I have different opinions than those I work with. I have different opinions with a lot of people. It doesn't mean that one of us is wrong.

Sometimes in a marriage, every area of disagreement automatically becomes a battle. The discussion becomes a competition with each partner trying to prove that they are right. Remember: it's okay to have different opinions. Now, there are times when you've got to come to agreement on decisions that need to be made, so those differences will need to be worked through. But we've got to drop this need to win fights, as well as the need to blame the other person. It's a trap that many couples fall into. Worry less about blame and more about resolution. Ultimately, what's more important: winning the fight or having harmony in your home? Would you rather be right or be happy?

Resolve Differences at Your Best Times

This one seems basic, but it's so critical. Fights get worse when you are tired or in a bad mood. I have to tell you, some of the worst fights in our marriage have been late at night. It's now 1 am, 2 am, and it went from a level two fight to a level eight or nine category fight just because of the time of day. We're bushed and we know we have to get up early. There may even be certain times of the month that are bad times for resolving disagreements (you know what I mean – work with me, people).

We'll make more sense to each other if we choose to talk things through at our best times. Schedule a time to work through your issues – a time that is good for both of you. Miscommunication gets resolved so much more quickly and peacefully when we are well rested and prepared to work at it together. Don't shoot yourself in the foot by adding bad timing to your list of frustrations.

Learning to communicate with your spouse, especially on hard topics, is a process. Yes, sometimes they make no sense at all. But be intentional and be gracious. Live out James 1:19 with God's help. With time, and with enough focus, we can learn to understand one another: maybe not perfectly, maybe not 100% of the time, but at least enough to get that couch through the door!

DISCUSSION STARTERS:

1. Who's the talker and who's the more silent one? Who's the better listener? Write out your answer and be prepared to discuss how you perceive each other.

2. What are your greatest limitations during harder conversations?

3. What are your pet peeves with your mate on how they interact during hard conversations? Write these here.

What God Says About Conflict Resolution:

1. **FORGIVE: We must live in the spirit of graciousness. To love well is to forgive well. God says we must forgive. That's His plan. Besides, bitterness will poison us and everyone else in our world. Instead, forgive as God forgave you – unconditionally! Then choose to let the offense go and not bring it up again.**

   Colossians 3:13 – Bear with each other and *forgive one another* if any of you has a grievance against someone. *Forgive as the Lord forgave you.*

   Ephesians 5:32 – Be kind and compassionate to one another, *forgiving each other*, just as in Christ God forgave you.

   1 Peter 4:8 – Most important of all, continue to show deep love for each other, for *love covers* a multitude of sins. NLT

   Proverbs 17:9 – Whoever would foster love *covers over* an offense, but whoever *repeats the matter separates close friends*.

2. **BE OTHERS-CENTERED: Marriage is the merging of two lives not the canceling of one. It's full on give and take. On one hand, you have to be willing to share your perspective, believing that your opinion matters. Speak up in love. On the other, you must respect and truly listen to your partner - really well.**

   2 Timothy 1:7 – For God has not given us *a spirit of fear and timidity*, but of power, love, and self-discipline. NLT

   Ephesians 4:15 – We will *speak the truth in love*…we will grow to become in every respect the mature body of him who is the head, that is, Christ.

   Philippians 2:3-4 – Do nothing out of selfish ambition or vain conceit. Rather, in humility *value others above yourselves, not looking to your own interests but each of you to the interests of the others.*

   1 Peter 3:8-10 – Finally, all of you, *be like-minded, be sympathetic, love one another, be compassionate and humble.* Do not repay evil with evil or insult with insult. On the contrary, repay evil with blessing, because to this you were called so that you may inherit a blessing. For, "Whoever would love life and see good days must keep their tongue from evil and their lips from deceitful speech.

3. **BE KIND: To resolve conflicts well, there is no place for anger or harsh treatment. How you talk to each other in times of stress and disagreement matters to God too. Anger in itself isn't wrong – it's how you handle it. Stay calm. Don't let things escalate. Let no unwholesome words come out of your mouth. There is no excuse for unkindness.**

41

Proverbs 22:24-25 – Do not make friends with a **hot-tempered person**, do not associate with **one easily angered**, or you may learn their ways and get yourself ensnared.

Ephesians 4:26 – In your anger do not sin: Do not let the sun go down while you are still angry…

Proverbs 15:1 – A gentle answer turns away wrath, but **a harsh word stirs up anger**.

James 1:19-20 – My dear brothers and sisters, take note of this: Everyone should be **quick to listen, slow to speak and slow to become angry**, because human anger does not produce the righteousness that God desires.

Ephesians 4:29-31 – **Do not let any unwholesome talk come out of your mouths**, but only what is helpful for building others up according to their needs, that it may benefit those who listen. [30] And do not grieve the Holy Spirit of God, with whom you were sealed for the day of redemption. [31] **Get rid of all bitterness, rage and anger, brawling and slander**, along with every form of malice.

4. **APOLOGIZE: Be willing to say sorry and make restitution where necessary. Don't downplay the need to get things right. Humble yourself. Admit you're wrong. No issue is more important than the relationship.**

Proverbs 14:9 – Fools **mock at making amends** for sin, but goodwill is found among the upright.

Proverbs 28:13 – Whoever conceals their sins does not prosper, but the one **who confesses and renounces** them finds mercy.

Matthew 5:23-24 – Therefore, if you remember that your brother or sister has something against you… **go and be reconciled** to them.

Matthew 18:15 – If your brother or sister sins, **go and point out their fault, just between the two of you**. If they listen to you, you have won them over.

James 5:16 – Therefore **confess your sins to each other** and pray for each other so that you may be healed. The prayer of a righteous [spouse] is powerful and effective.

Romans 12:17-19 – Do not repay anyone evil for evil. Be careful to do what is right in the eyes of everyone. [18] If it is possible, as far as it depends on you, live at peace with everyone. [19] Do not take revenge, my dear friends, but leave room for God's wrath, for it is written: "It is mine to avenge; I will repay," says the Lord.

2 Corinthians 13:11 – Finally, brothers and sisters, rejoice! **Strive for full restoration**, encourage one another, be of one mind, live in peace. And the God of love and peace will be with you.

Chapter 9
Anchored for Life:
Growing Together Spiritually
Dr. Dave Currie

Donalyn and I have stayed strong in our marital and faith climb for nearly fifty years. Many times, we are asked these kinds of deepening questions. What has anchored us spiritually? What are the secrets of our shared faith climb? How do we stay so anchored to the Lord and each other year after year?

The following guiding principles are our *'non-negotiables'* of faith that have secured us all these years. While many other activities, disciplines and events have come and gone in our spiritual lives over the years, these ones have been the common ropes that have fastened us irrevocably to what is truly significant. These are the six spiritual perspectives that have anchored our spiritual climb.

1. Keep a soft heart toward God.
We have committed to each other – actually promised – that we will show our love for each other by keeping our own faith alive and growing. Donalyn keeps her faith strong. I keep mine strong. The most important aspect of this is a soft and listening heart to the Lord that willingly responds to the Holy Spirit's promptings. Ask God to remove any resemblance of a heart of stone (a hard and indifferent heart) and give you a heart of flesh (a soft and responsive heart) (Ezekiel 11:19-20*).* That will change everything! We consistently strive to give our lives and marriage to the Lord in prayer – making Him the center of our home. As part of our commitment to each other, we each choose to read our Bibles daily with that same sensitive, listening heart. It's amazing how God speaks to me about my stupidity in how I might be treating Donalyn or the kids. Soft hearts listen. We have it on our walls at home, joining Joshua, *"As for me and my house, we will serve the Lord"* (Joshua 24:15).

2. You can't change your spouse, so quit trying!
I don't know if you see what I see, but in observing many couples, I can see I am not alone. First, we marry someone opposite us. This is normal and truly a universal phenomenon. But then, we spend the rest of our lives trying to make our spouse be like us, think like us and agree with us. Dumb. It's like we have an insatiable need to have them see and do life our way. That push to change our spouse never goes well. I'm in trouble for admitting this, but I couldn't begin to tell you how many ways I have tried to change Donalyn over the years – some subtle and some… well, let's say not so subtle. But Jesus said that we shouldn't worry about the speck in our spouse's eye when we have a plank in our own (Matthew 7:3-5). So, stop trying. You simply can't change them. After all, it is not your job to do that, it's God's. Focus on letting God deeply and completely change you. You'd think after almost five decades of marriage that I'd be close to fully adjusted, but no… a lot of change is still needed. Just ask Donalyn.

3. Pray together.

I know. Nothing new. We all should be praying – alone and together. This is not profound. But what we know and what we do are usually very different. Simple, straight question: *"Do you pray with your spouse each day?"* (Answer honestly). That's the point. Almost without exception, most couples who call themselves Christians don't pray together let alone doing it daily. Start tonight. Join with us everyday to invite God into your lives and activities together. And beyond these day-to-day concerns and joys we share with Him, we take our apprehensions to Him regarding major transitions, work pressures, location moves, adding children and all other significant changes or challenges we face. We pray daily for our kids and grandkids. We also pray with each other and for each other. Practically, we always hold hands when we go to God in prayer. We have since before we were married. After all, if you can't grab your mate's hand to pray, then get things right so you can! You may want to try a weekly time of prayer where we get on our knees together to go to war for what really matters – a more comprehensive prayer session. And yes, a family that prays together really does stay together.

4. Live Jesus at home.

Following Jesus is a 24/7 commitment. Sunday Christians make shallow partners, inconsistent parents and convey a double message to their children. Faith at home is a real faith not a fabricated one designed to create an image for onlookers. To live your faith within the four walls of your household is so critical to transferring faith to the next generation – your own kids. We believe you can't be sensitive to God and insensitive to people – especially those closest you. Jesus has to be Lord at home. And once you have authentically walked it, then you will feel free and more comfortable about genuinely talking about it. We were intentional. We shared our faith up close and personal with our kids using teachable moments every day as they came up. We simplified our family faith message to this guiding motto: *Put God First – Life Goes Best.* Our kids all embraced this and boy, are we forever grateful!

5. Don't skip church.

Having pastored in five different congregations over the years, I had the natural vantage point to witness something firsthand. Going to church regularly doesn't guarantee a person stays connected to Jesus, but I promise you, nothing good ever comes out of missing church repeatedly. The lesson is clear: *If you skip, you slip*. We are warned about neglecting the assembling with other believers and to continue encouraging one another within a faith community (Hebrews 10:25). Jesus confirmed that He loved the church and was committed to building His church (Matthew 16:18). Ok, I know that some churches have issues. But don't make excuses. Find a good church that really teaches the Bible. Plug in. Engage. Grow. Persevere. Stay there. Don't miss. We're thirty-three years now going to our church. God has taught us so much.

6. Make a difference together.

The final spiritual anchor has to do with doing Kingdom service together. But the key is joint, simultaneous expressions of God's love. There's nothing like helping others as a couple. It builds great relational and spiritual connection. And as the kids get older, it's so enriching to put your shoulders to the same wheel together with them too. Everybody grows closer to God and each other when this happens. What are we talking about? Here's a taste of how Donalyn and I have served together over the years. We have led care groups, taught Sunday School and organized youth groups and mission trips. We've spoken at retreats, taught premarital preparation, served in marriage ministry and counseled and prayed with many couples. We've hosted many people in our home, held neighborhood Bible Studies and helped with work projects both in our community and overseas. Now you have the feel. Do something with your mate to make a difference that puts a smile not only on your faces and the people you serve but also on God's face as well. This really takes you deeper in your faith.

So, there you go. These six anchors have really worked personally for us in our spiritual climb. We hope as you consider trying them that they will help you grow together spiritually as much as they have us. Keep letting God anchor you growing deeper with Him and each other.

DISCUSSION STARTERS:

1. Which are the Spiritual Anchors that you two are stronger on and which are the ones you are weaker on? Identify both your couple strengths and weaknesses spiritually.
   - Spiritual Couple Strengths:

   - Spiritual Couple Weaknesses:

2. Why do you think that your spiritual life seems to slip or fade in importance in your individual and collective lives? Share what you feel are the three most common reasons for faith fade in your life or marriage.
   -
   -
   -

3. What would be two good steps to take to renew your faith journey as a couple?
   -
   -

What God Says About Convictions:

1. **True wisdom in life begins with putting God first. When we say, "Jesus is Lord" and live with Him calling the shots, we are on our way to experiencing life as God intended. Our priorities change. This will greatly impact your marriage.**

   Prov. 3:5,6 – *Trust in the LORD with all your heart*; do not depend on your own understanding. **Seek his will in all you do,** and he will show you which path to take. NLT

   Matt. 6:33 – **Seek the Kingdom of God above all else,** and live righteously, and he will give you everything you need. NLT

   Eccles 12:13 – After all this, there is *only one thing to say: Have reverence for God,* and obey his commands, because this is all that we were created for. GNT

   Proverbs 1:7 – To have knowledge, you *must first have reverence for the LORD*. Stupid people have no respect for wisdom and refuse to learn. GNT

   Psalm 127:1-2 – *Unless the LORD builds a house*; the work of the builders is wasted. Unless the LORD protects a city, guarding it with sentries will do no good.
   ^{2} It is useless for you to work so hard from early morning until late at night, anxiously working for food to eat; for God gives rest to his loved ones. NLT

2. **God wants our best. He rewards us for sincerely seeking Him. His plan for our life and marriage - for all of our lives – is better than you could create on your own. We need to trust His plan.**

   John 10:10 – The thief comes only to steal and kill and destroy; I have come that *they may have life, and have it to the full.*

   Hebrews 11:6 – And without faith it is impossible to please God, because anyone who comes to him must believe that he exists and that *he rewards those who earnestly seek him.*

   Psalm 37:4 – Take delight in the LORD, and *he will give you the desires of your heart.*

   Psalm 84:11 – For the LORD God is a sun and shield; *the LORD bestows favor and honor; no good thing does he withhold from those whose walk is blameless.*

   I Timothy 6:17 – Command those who are rich in this present world not to be arrogant nor to put their hope in wealth, which is so uncertain, but to put their hope in God, *who richly provides us with everything for our enjoyment.*

Jer. 29:11 – For I know the plans I have for you," declares the LORD, *"plans to prosper you and not to harm you, plans to give you hope and a future.*

3. **Jesus can be our internal anchor. He promises to be our strength and guide through all life's challenging circumstances. God and I need to be inseparable. I grow to rely and depend on Him.**

    Heb. 6:19 – We have this hope as *an anchor for the soul, firm and secure*.

    Phil. 4:13 – I have *the strength to face all conditions* by the power that Christ gives me. GNT

    Hebrews 4:16 – Let us have confidence, then, and approach God's throne, where there is grace. There we will receive mercy and find *grace to help us just when we need it.* GNT

    1 Peter 5:7 – *Give all your worries and cares to God*, for he cares about you. NLT

    Phil. 4:6-7 – Don't worry about anything; instead, pray about everything. Tell God what you need, and thank him for all he has done. [7] *Then you will experience God's peace*, which exceeds anything we can understand. His *peace will guard your hearts and minds* as you live in Christ Jesus.

4. **Trusting Jesus brings change – He'll change you and impact your marriage. The shaping of our character and our values are based on His call to holiness and His strength to live the difference knowing God makes.**

    2 Cor. 5:17 – This means that anyone who belongs to Christ has *become a new person*. The old life is gone; *a new life has begun*! NLT

    1 John 2: 5-6 – But if anyone obeys his word, love for God is truly made complete in them. This is how we know we are in him: [6] Whoever claims to live in him **must live as Jesus did.**

    Phil 2:13 – For God is working in you, *giving you the desire and the power to do what pleases him.* NLT

    Micah 6:8 – No, O people, the LORD has told you what is good, and this is what he requires of you: to *do what is right, to love mercy, and to walk humbly with your God*. NLT

    Romans 12:1-2 – And so, dear brothers, I plead with you to give your bodies to God. *Let them be a living sacrifice, holy—the kind he can accept.* When you think of what he has done for you, is this too much to ask? [2] Don't copy the behavior and customs of this world, but *be a new and different person with a fresh newness in all you do and think*. Then you will learn from your own experience how his ways will really satisfy you. TLB

5. **Your faith must positively impact your primary relationships. Faith must hit home. You can't be sensitive to God and insensitive to people. You can't be right with God without being right with your spouse as well.**

   1 John 1:7 – But if we are living in the light of God's presence, just as Christ does, then **we have wonderful fellowship and joy with each other**, and the blood of Jesus his Son cleanses us from every sin. TLB

   1 Timothy 5:8 – Anyone who does not **provide for** their relatives, and **especially for their own household,** has denied the faith and is worse than an unbeliever.

   1 Corinthians 7:33-34 – But a married man is concerned about the affairs of this world—**how he can please his wife**—and his interests are divided. An unmarried woman is concerned about the Lord's affairs: Her aim is to be devoted to the Lord in both body and spirit. But a married woman is concerned about the affairs of this world—**how she can please her husband.**

   1 Peter 3:7 – Husbands, in the same way **be considerate as you live with your wives**, and **treat them with respect** as the weaker partner and as heirs with you of the gracious gift of life, so that nothing will hinder your prayers.

   Eccles. 4:12 – A **cord of three strands** is not quickly broken. Agree to braid God into your marriage.

Chapter 10
It Starts With You:
Personal Spiritual Training
Jody Wandzura

While working toward a Kinesiology degree at university, I landed a part-time job at a fitness center. In my fourth year, several individuals approached me to design an exercise program for them. Since this enriched my learning, I spent hours creating a personal training manual explaining the basics of getting fit through cardiovascular exercise and strength training. I proudly presented the manual to each client, expecting great results! Months passed, and I didn't see any improvements in their appearance. I soon realized that merely handing them a manual did not guarantee results. These people wanted magic to happen, hoping their jiggles and rolls would disappear.

Upon reflection, I discovered a key concept: "Unless you are willing to put in the time and intentional effort, all of this personal training talk will be worthless." The clients had the manual and read it but just didn't follow it. The foundational problem wasn't the knowledge but the motivation to follow through. They didn't fully grasp the life-giving benefits of exercise that come when you put in the work. They also hadn't experienced the perks of a disciplined lifestyle, a sense of accomplishment, and pride in themselves. I felt compelled to add an opening section in my manual titled "The Rewards of Exercise."

Personal Spiritual Training is similar; people want to pray and have all their problems disappear. The same key concept applies: "Unless you are willing to put in the time and intentional effort, all of this personal (spiritual) training talk will be worthless." What does it mean to put in time and intentional effort? God says, "Draw near to me, and I will draw near to you" (James 4:8). He also says, "If you love me, keep my commands" (John 14:15). The more I love God, the more I will obey Him. I must work hard to do what he says and to incorporate meaningful spiritual disciplines.

What are the key commands that God has in the Bible? God says to love others, even if they don't deserve it. God says to apologize when you sin, and He will forgive you. God says if you confess that Jesus is Lord and believe in Him, you will be saved. God says to be strong in the Lord, resist the devil, and he will flee from you. God asks us to be generous as He has been generous with us. God says to trust Him, and then we will have peace. God asks us to take up His cross and follow Him, giving us purpose in life. Salvation. Love. Forgiveness. Freedom. Generosity. Peace. Purpose. These are the results of drawing near and obeying God.

My dad created our family's mantra when I was young: "Put God First — Life Goes Best." Once you understand the value of this statement, you will hopefully have the motivation to put in the time and intentional effort to grow in your faith. Placing God first will mold you into the most fantastic spouse, friend, sibling, parent, and neighbor. Like the personal training manual I created for physical fitness, below is the equivalent of personal training in *spiritual* fitness.

Personal Spiritual Training Manual

There is no secret to spiritual growth; you must spend time daily with God by including these five critical components:

1. talking to God (prayer)
2. hearing from God (reading His Word or waiting on God)
3. learning from God (journaling on what you are reading or writing out your prayers)
4. worshiping God (in music or serving)
5. sharing God (telling others about him)

Talking to God

Prayer is talking to God. It is as simple as talking to a friend or a mentor. There are times when I chat with Him throughout my day and times of focused crying out to Him. Regardless of the kind of prayer we are discussing, it is integral to growing closer to God.

When a friend was learning about prayer, I remember her saying, "But I don't know what to say!" God isn't worried about our words. He wants to hear our hearts and to spend time with us; He wants us to be honest with him with our thoughts and feelings. When I was a little kid, my Sunday School leader taught me an acronym I still use when praying. Maybe it will help you, too. ACTS stands for Adoration, Confession, Thankfulness, and Supplication.

> **Adoration**. I start by praising God and telling him how wonderful He is. It usually begins with the phrase, "I praise you for…" When I spend my time and energy remembering how amazing God is, a greater sense of respect, awe, and reverence develops in my life. It reminds me that God is God, and I am not. It reminds me that He has saved me from death, so I owe Him everything. It reminds me that he is all-knowing, all-powerful, and in control even when my life seems to be heading toward doom and gloom. It reminds me that I need to praise God more often to keep my heart focused on Him.

> **Confession**. When I was a child, my parents taught me to apologize to someone when I did wrong to them, so why do I rarely remember to confess to God for those same things? For example, if I lie to someone, I apologize for lying. Too often, I stop there. I also need to go to God and say sorry to Him for breaking His ninth commandment, saying, "I'm sorry for…" When I bring my shortcomings to God, it reminds me that I am sinful and need God's strength and the Holy Spirit's power. I am brought to my spiritual knees, asking for forgiveness.

> **Thankfulness**. It is easy to thank God for all his blessings in our lives. We have so much to be thankful for – we just have to look. I have learned that thankfulness comes from your perspective.

> - My Life Group leader from our church prayed, "God, thank you for all the good times and bad times. Thank you for everything you have given us and things we do not have." I liked her perspective!
> - Another friend prayed, "Thank You for letting us go bankrupt so we could learn to DEPEND on You for everything." That prayer brought tears to my eyes.

- When he was five, my son prayed, "Thank You, God, for making all the wonderful people I see." That five-year-old's prayer helped me remember that the same Creator who made me in His image created all people.

When I am thankful, my walk with God, daily outlook and overall life improve. I challenge you to read the book *One Thousand Gifts*; it opened my eyes to the amazing world around me.

Supplication. God wants us to come to Him with our needs because he loves us and wants to care for us. Unfortunately, we focus too much on getting our desires met. We are needy people, or should I say "wanty" people. We continuously ask for more "stuff." We pray for popularity, promotion and power in the eyes of the world. We demand God to take away difficulties to make our lives easier. We get stuck in a selfish rut of wanting God to act like our personal genie. Perhaps the solution is to balance our prayer time between the four areas; then, we would be more in awe, more humble, more content and less worried.

Hearing from God

Conversation is supposed to be a two-way deal, but I spend more time speaking to God than listening. Only once in my life have I heard an audible voice telling me what to do, so what are other ways I hear from Him? The Bible is the easiest method for me to glean from God as those are His words. Different ways to hear from Him are through people who are mature in their faith and can speak wisdom to me. Sometimes, just being out in nature, I am in awe of God's breathtaking creation and am still before him.

Often, as I have grown closer to God, I get promptings in my heart. I feel that I need to pull my car over and ask if someone is okay. I stop in the mall and talk to a lady sitting on a bench because I feel God wants me to. If I am unsure if the prompting is from God, I check that it aligns with His Word before I take that step of faith.

Learning from God

A hand-in-hand combo to hearing from God is learning from Him. When I read the Bible on its own, I uncover rich treasure, but minutes later, those golden nuggets are buried in the back of my mind – rarely to be remembered again! The best way to recall God's Word is to write it down. I have been trying to journal over the past few years, and it is in the writing that I have started to remember, learn, and then apply what I hear from God. Then, a step further is to have someone keep me accountable to apply the changes God wants me to make. I want to be a learner of the Word all my life.

Worshiping God

We all worship or live for something. I want to live my life in a way entirely devoted to God. I want to love God more than my family, more than my spouse, and more than my kids. Anything or anyone I put before my relationship with God could become like an idol in my life as I do what they want (or even what I desire) and not always what God wants.

Another way to intentionally worship God is through music. So many amazing songs glorify God and bring me to a place where my spirit connects with God in profound ways that I cannot explain. As my heart aligns with Him, I grow in my desire to obey.

Sharing God

I come alive when discussing God's life-changing difference. I recall one time when my faith was extensively tested. My neighbor was asking questions about God, so we decided to go for coffee. I forgot how hard it was to hear her in a noisy environment. For her to listen to me, I had to speak at the volume one would use for a crowd of 100 students in a gym without a microphone. Everyone in the coffee shop was literally staring at me while I shared about Jesus' love, the salvation of the cross, and God's plan for her life. I will never forget that day and how terrified I felt, but I still wonder how many people heard about Jesus for the first time!

I also remember when I shared with a parent on my daughter's soccer team, and he was shocked that "normal people still follow that God stuff". I laughed and told him how the Bible speaks to me and continues changing my life. I added that the Bible could change his life, too. He said, "Fine, I will read it if you get me one." I leave every conversation about God with my heart racing and a smile on my face!

So, are you up for this personal training challenge? If you are willing to engage in some of these things to grow closer to God, I bet they will dramatically change your relationships, perspective, and life for the better! Your marriage will prosper. Your spouse will thank you. It starts with you.

DISCUSSION STARTERS:

1. When you pray, do you follow any routine or pattern, or what do most of your prayers entail?

2. In what ways do you best hear and learn from God?

3. Share a memory of when you spent time fully worshiping God or when you intentionally shared Jesus with someone. How did you feel in that moment?

Chapter 11
Loving in 3D:
Understanding Lasting Marital Intimacy
Dr. Dave Currie

Intimacy has been warmly but accurately defined as *"into-me-see"*. The human heart is made for connection; we crave knowing another and being known. It is deciding to let the partner "see into me." It is not a one-way deal either. It is mutual. That is why marriage is so unique, as it requires two people who are both vulnerable in disclosure and trustworthy in action to keep the intimacy growing. Your spouse should be the one person that you share everything with!

That leads to this simple but powerful concept that we embrace called **Loving in "3D."** We try to live this and pass it on to you. Beyond spiritual centeredness, our deep and personal *faith in God that anchors us*, it involves focusing on three dimensions within marriage to create something extraordinary. It includes Relational Companionship, Emotional Closeness and Sexual Connection. We have witnessed over the years that when all three aspects consistently and caringly become central to our regular life cycle, our primary relationship grows more satisfying and sustainable. And that's what we all desire.

The three dimensions of a great marriage covered below revolve around one assumption: **Jesus is the middle of your life and marriage, and He is your spiritual anchor.** If this is true, you should:

- **Build a Vibrant Faith:** Decide that you want Jesus in the center of your life and marriage. Surrender today.

- **Live Out Your Faith:** Daily, become more like Jesus: regular prayer, reading his Word and honest faith discussions.

- **Change as a Spouse:** Employing the Fruit of the Spirit (Galatians 5:22-23) or the Love Chapter (1 Corinthians 13:4-7), and living for Jesus at home so He improves how you treat your spouse.

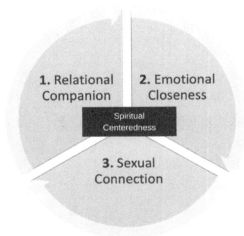

The **Loving in "3D"** Diagram shows the three dimensions and how they cycle together:

Relational Companionship is the art of being friends and staying friends. It mirrors the time of your premarital dating period when we had fun doing things together. It includes romance, special occasions, simple and crazy activities, and sharing lots of smiles. It's doing a lot of life, side-by-side. It's a true sense of life togetherness.

Relational companionship is our warmth in friendship. It is what makes us smile and what we enjoy about the other person. We cherish their company, and we like who they are. We laugh together, talk forever and can't get enough of each other. We care less about what we do and more about just being together. We put in great effort to create memories. We like what the other person brings out in us and how they make us feel. We can't imagine life without them.

Relational intimacy requires time spent together – "us time." We could do almost anything, but some ideas create stronger connections. What works best for you? Watching TV together or walking on the beach? Biking or hiking? Playing cards or going to the movies? What do you and your mate like to do together that builds into your friendship? Playing creates fun, lightheartedness and revitalization. It keeps your relational spark alive and fans your attraction.

But, you simply need to keep this *"us time"* going. You can't let it slip. Kids and work have to make way for carving out regular dates to keep on being real companions – a minimum of twice per month of two to three hours alone. If you have no kids yet, aim at getting out once per week. That's right. You can't stay home more than one in four dates. And, your outgoing doesn't have to cost you. By the way, try to limit "Dinner and a Movie" option to one in four dates. Get out of any ruts and keep the laughter, playfulness, and your brand of silliness happening. Take the time to connect.

Emotional Closeness is the sense of being fully known and still loved. When the marriage is strong – nobody knows you like your mate! It involves authentically and mutually sharing at a deeper level and, in so doing, building solid trust. It's learning things together – *face-to-face* – so that you have a place where you feel understood, respected, validated, and appreciated. Your relationship is safe for both of you. Your hearts bond, and as trusted confidantes, you enjoy a true sense of life collaboration.

Emotional closeness is accepting each other as we are. As you build into your relational connection with dating, you naturally will learn more about each other, including your *GBUs* – the good, the bad, and the ugly. We are all GBU package deals, as none of us is perfect. Who we are shows up in our opinions and values. Our care for a hurting friend. Our indifference to exercise. Our lack of patience for incompetence. Our habit of being late. Our desire to make the world a better place. Our love for money. Our eye for design. And the list goes on! Although you ultimately want to increase your good things and minimize your ugly, you are a unique package, and so is your spouse.

Emotional closeness is the personal choice of discussing some of your life's most profound questions. Who am I? How do I feel about myself? What are my greatest hopes or biggest fears? What are my likes and dislikes? What critical events in my life have shaped me? What makes me "me"? Would you share your answers with everyone, anyone, or no one? As you get to know each other, you earn trust, and sharing your answers to some of these questions gets easier. Within this, you feel the freedom to be honest and connect deeply. No judgment. No condemnation. No drama. Just trust. This safe place is critical to emotional closeness; vulnerability may seem too risky without it.

Emotional closeness can also come through praying together. As you pray with and for each other daily, it can become an intentional way to be vulnerable in more profound issues. You each share how you are doing, your concerns, praise reports, trials, and fears. Together, you can bring these cares to the Lord.

Growing emotional closeness anchors relational confidence, and genuine care must not fade. You must prioritize your relationship by continuing to put your spouse first. Kindness has to rule. Thoughtfulness and consideration must be maintained. Your marriage has to be an **"anger-free zone."** You will have to learn to manage difficult emotions. No excuses. Harshness, the opposite of warmth, kills closeness. So, when frustrations do arise, own your stuff, work to resolve things quicker and forgive sooner.

To stay close emotionally, which is often easier for one spouse over the other, you have to create time to share yourself and equally to listen. Try two to three times each week, where for about twenty minutes, you open up with each other. How are we doing? How is your life going? No distractions. No people. No cell phones or TV. If you need help with what questions you could be talking about, get our *Date Night Discussion Starters* off Dr. Dave's website, Doing Family Right. Get alone face-to-face. Period. Take time to create closeness.

Sexual Connection is the ultimate act of total transparency. Sexual oneness is a journey of discovery as a couple. What general knowledge you think you might know about sex before marriage still has to be worked out with a real person after the wedding. Great passion in the bedroom has to be about mutuality. Both partners must be engaged and enthralled. It's about enjoying great feelings together as bodies unite. It's the *heart-to-heart* experience and a true sense of life intimacy. It's making love not having sex.

When a husband and wife enjoy a mutually satisfying sexual relationship, it creates physical closeness. It is God's plan, and it is incredible! One man. One woman. For life. Unfortunately, our world has twisted this concept and watered it down.

You will enjoy experiencing the most intimate connection with your spouse in marriage. It will require that you learn about them and find out what pleases them. Your attitude towards each other requires saying, "I want to put your needs before mine. *I want to learn to please you."* Our goal should be to serve our spouse – even in bed! When you are focused on pleasing the other person, you are on your way to incredible sexual intimacy.

Sexual intimacy before marriage.

The greatest gift you can give your spouse is your innocence. Did you get that? It says that I saved myself for you. It shows value. It demotes comparison and insecurity and promotes exclusivity and worth. Many counselors agree that sexual intimacy is best when shared with one person for life. You don't want to give yourself away to multiple partners for many reasons: emotional (feeling used), mental (memories of others get brought into your future marriage), health (STIs) and relational (not feeling special). Just you. Just me. An exclusive gift of purity.

For those who have already had sexual experiences with others, there is still a way forward for a healthy marriage together. Retaining increased sexual freedom requires essential conversations with God, a counselor and future spouse. God is in the business of redeeming lives and making all things new again. If your sexual experiences have been with pain or regret, it would be helpful to talk to a Christian counselor who can help you deal with this hurtful baggage so you don't bring it into your future marriage.

So, until you are married, just enjoy being together. Enjoy relational intimacy and play together. Develop emotional connections and begin praying together. Appreciate each other's company, focus on your friendship and trust each other with your feelings, but leave the sexual relationship where God designed it to be. You will never regret saving sexual intimacy for after the wedding.

Sexual intimacy after marriage

There's a lot to work through in your marital sex life: frequency, variation, initiation, exclusiveness, and satisfaction for both of you, to name a few. Enjoy the chapters on sexual intimacy to go deeper in your discussion and your closeness.

Remember, faithfulness matters, and "what happens in Vegas" – doesn't stay in Vegas. It destroys many marriages. Make your mate your only love target. Begin talking about your level of mutuality and pleasure. Simply ask your spouse. "What would make sex better for you?" Listen closely. It may take time to connect sexually – but keep leaning in so it becomes great for both of you.

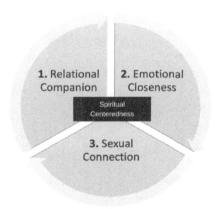

Look again at the diagram. Do you see the **ARROWS**? Their implied motion tells us a lot as they circle the three dimensions. You must continuously rotate through all three aspects to get true marital intimacy. You can't leave one section of the cycle out of the rotation and expect to have a healthy, balanced marriage.

Keep being a playful companion, keep being a trusted confidante and keep being a passionate lover. Set a time to discuss how well you are doing at LOVING IN 3D. Seek the Lord together on what steps you must take as a couple.

Dreaming up the perfect picture of marital intimacy involves relational connections, emotional vulnerability and mutually satisfying sex. It says, "You are the only one for me," and it is authentic *"into-me-see."*

DISCUSSION STARTERS:

1. Score out of 10 how you feel you are doing as a couple on the Three Dimensions:
   - Relational Companionship: /10

   - Emotional Closeness: /10

   - Sexual Connection: /10

2. Which area are you the worst at? What steps can you take to improve YOUR part of the equation?

3. Suggest and then agree on one commitment you can make as a couple to improve each dimension in the next three to four months.

What God Says About Closeness:

Read together, share your observations and discuss implications to your marriage.

- **Genesis 2:24-25** – *This explains why a man leaves his father and mother and is joined to his wife, and the two are united into one. Now the man and his wife were both naked, but they felt no shame.* NLT

- **1 Corinthians 7:2-5** – *But because there is so much sexual immorality, each man should have his own wife, and each woman should have her own husband. The husband should fulfill his wife's sexual needs, and the wife should fulfill her husband's needs. The wife gives authority over her body to her husband, and the husband gives authority over his body to his wife. Do not deprive each other of sexual relations, unless you both agree to refrain from sexual intimacy for a limited time so you can give yourselves more completely to prayer. Afterward, you should come together again so that Satan won't be able to tempt you because of your lack of self-control.* NLT

- **Hebrews 13:4** – *Marriage should be honored by all, and the marriage bed kept pure, for God will judge the adulterer and all the sexually immoral.*

- **Matthew 5:27-28** – *You have heard the commandment that says, 'You must not commit adultery.' But I say, anyone who even looks at a woman with lust has already committed adultery with her in his heart.* NLT

- **Proverbs 5:15-21** – *Drink water from your own well—share your love only with your wife. Why spill the water of your springs in the streets, having sex with just anyone? You should reserve it for yourselves. Never share it with strangers. Let your wife be a fountain of blessing for you. Rejoice in the wife of your youth. She is a loving deer, a graceful doe. Let her breasts satisfy you always. May you always be captivated by her love. Why be captivated, my son, by an immoral woman, or fondle the breasts of a promiscuous woman? For the LORD sees clearly what a man does, examining every path he takes.* NLT

- **1 Thessalonians 4:3-7** – *God's will is for you to be holy, so stay away from all sexual sin.* [4] *Then each of you will control his own body[b] and live in holiness and honor—* [5] *not in lustful passion like the pagans who do not know God and his ways.* [6] *Never harm or cheat a fellow believer in this matter by violating his wife,[c] for the Lord avenges all such sins, as we have solemnly warned you before.* [7] *God has called us to live holy lives, not impure lives.* NLT

- ***Romans 13:13-14*** – Let us behave decently, as in the daytime, not in carousing and drunkenness, not in sexual immorality and debauchery, not in dissension and jealousy. [14] Rather, clothe yourselves with the Lord Jesus Christ, and do not think about how to gratify the desires of the flesh.[a]

- **2 Tim. 2:22** – Flee the evil desires of youth and pursue righteousness, faith, love and peace, along with those who call on the Lord out of a pure heart.

- **Ephesians 5:3-7** – But among you there must not be even a hint of sexual immorality, or of any kind of impurity, or of greed, because these are improper for God's holy people. [4] Nor should there be obscenity, foolish talk or coarse joking, which are out of place, but rather thanksgiving. [5] For of this you can be sure: No immoral, impure or greedy person—such a person is an idolater—has any inheritance in the kingdom of Christ and of God.[a] [6] Let no one deceive you with empty words, for because of such things God's wrath comes on those who are disobedient. [7] Therefore do not be partners with them.

- **The PASSIONATE LOVERS of the Song of Solomon:**
  Kiss me and kiss me again, for your love is sweeter than wine. How fragrant your cologne; your name is like its spreading fragrance. Take me with you; come, let's run! The king has brought me into his bedroom.
  You are beautiful, my darling, beautiful beyond words.
  You are so handsome, my love, pleasing beyond words!
  Your love delights me, my treasure, my bride. Your love is better than wine. You are my private garden, my treasure, my bride, a secluded spring, a hidden fountain.
  My lover is mine, and I am his. Blow on my garden and spread its fragrance all around. Come into your garden, my love; taste its finest fruits.
  I have entered my garden, my treasure, my bride! I gather myrrh with my spice and eat honeycomb with my honey. I drink wine with my milk.
  Oh, lover and beloved, eat and drink! Yes, drink deeply of your love! My lover is dark and dazzling, better than ten thousand others! I am my lover's, and my lover is mine.
  You are beautiful, my darling, yes, as beautiful as Jerusalem, as majestic as an army with billowing banners. Turn your eyes away, for they overpower me.
  I am my lover's, and he claims me as his own. When my lover looks at me, he is delighted with what he sees.
  Oh, how beautiful you are! How pleasing, my love, how full of delights. You are slender like a palm tree, and your breasts are like its clusters of fruit. I said, "I will climb the palm tree and take hold of its fruit." May your breasts be like grape clusters, and the fragrance of your breath like apples. May your kisses be as exciting as the best wine, flowing gently over lips and teeth.
  Come, my love, let us go out to the fields and spend the night among the wildflowers. There I will give you my love, new delights as well as old, which I have saved for you, my lover.
  Even among countless young women, I would still choose my dove, my perfect one.
  Place me like a seal over your heart, like a seal on your arm. For love is as strong as death, its jealousy as enduring as the grave. Love flashes like fire, the brightest kind of flame. Many waters cannot quench love, nor can rivers drown it. If a man tried to buy love with all his wealth, his offer would be utterly scorned. You have captured my heart, my treasure, my bride. You hold it hostage with one glance of your eyes.   *Selected text from Song of Solomon

- **Titus 2:11-13** – For the grace of God has appeared that offers salvation to all people. [12] It teaches us to say "No" to ungodliness and worldly passions, and to live self-controlled, upright and godly lives in this present age, [13] while we wait for the blessed hope.

Chapter 12
Coming Clean:
Facing the Truth About Who You Are
Dr. Dave Currie

When I was young, say ages four to eight, my mother would warn me – actually more like threaten me (add Mom's cross tone of voice) – *"Don't you dare lie to me! I will always find out!"* I remember feeling a very serious check in my spirit that guided my choices because I had this eerie dread that she had some kind of sixth sense that 'just knew' when I was lying. Maybe you can relate.

I remember later in life learning in Sunday School – ***"BE SURE YOUR SINS WILL FIND YOU OUT!"*** This reinforced that whatever I did secretly in hope that I would not get caught, would still eventually surface. The truth would ultimately come out.

What I was taught early is a very solid reflection of what Scripture says. Wise Solomon says, "He who covers His sin will not prosper, but the one who confesses and renounces them finds mercy" (Proverbs 28:13). Don't try to hide your sin and selfishness. Living with secrets will hurt you. It is always better to "Come Clean".

Jesus states this truth even more directly and likely the verse behind the phrase: "Be sure your sins will find you out." He said, "There is nothing concealed that will not be disclosed, or hidden that will not be made known. What you have said in the dark will be heard in the daylight, and what you have whispered in the ear in the inner rooms will be proclaimed from the roofs" (Luke 12:2,3). The truth is, what's done or said in secret will be exposed. Count on it.

We'd be wise not to mess with any of God's principles for life. This one is very clear and it's not just for our children. For all of us – the mandate is undeniable. Don't lie. No half-truths, no misleading, no minimizing and no withholding! Telling the truth to people in the first place and then coming clean when we don't is clearly God's plan. The arrogant cannot stand comfortably in His presence. He hates all who do wrong; He destroys those who tell lies (Psalm 5:5,6). He calls us to "keep our tongue from evil and our lips from telling lies" (Psalm 34:13). Truth-speaking is one of the ten commandments (Exodus 20:16).

In spite of God's strong directive, we recognize something VERY different in our culture. We hear "What they don't know won't hurt them" or "It's okay as long as you don't get caught!" Maybe the most famous dismissal of trust and truth is: "What happens in Vegas – stays in Vegas". People argue that it's ok if others don't find out. So they compromise, cheat, spend, flirt, drink, gamble, indulge and a host of other moral and relational failures, selfishly maintaining they can get away with it. They feel they can lie their way through it.

Others prefer to reason that by not telling the truth to those closest to us – especially our spouse – we are doing the loving thing. We don't want to hurt them. We say we don't want to wreck the relationship. That's a ton of self-deception! We forget that our actions and words already have violated the trust – we have already really hurt them.

I hear this type of thinking a lot – especially when it comes to serious breaches of trust in a marriage – like affairs, private porn use, flirting with others or spending money secretly. This view of withholding is foolish thinking. Through over forty-eight years of helping people and calling people to greatness in surrender to Jesus Christ, the importance of truth and trust rings out. Nearly every day, I'm in the trenches with hurting people working through a myriad of life mistakes and the lies connected to them. We shouldn't be surprised that my experience on what ends up working best for a person is what God has said all along. Simply put – don't lie. Tell the truth. When you mislead, come clean and be honest for the good of all and as soon as possible.

Why Come Clean

The benefits of coming clean are extensive. Here are a few of the more significant reasons to move quickly into full confession and honesty:

- **To Re-Establish Your Spiritual Walk.** Our sin separates us from God. Our confession honors the Lord. His forgiveness creates a sense of well-being with our Maker. We feel humbled but free again to approach Him. Coming clean brings freedom with God and allows us to move forward in our faith journey. And coming clean with God but not coming clean with the people you hurt, doesn't work.

- **To Discontinue Spousal Betrayal.** Our lies traumatize our mate. Trust is the foundation of any great relationship. Our withholding hurts our spouse and our lying and denial creates a cavern between you. Stopping the lies will stop the perpetual wounding over and over again and the beginning of healing is possible.

- **To Break the Lying Cycle.** Lying has become easier and easier. It's how you operate. But the ongoing masterminding of deceit is exhausting. It becomes a non-stop hamster-wheel. More lies have to be created to cover previous lies. It's taxing to have to keep track of non-truth you have said before. Speaking the truth is freeing.

- **To Lift the Burden of Deception.** Lying crushes us. We bear the inner pain of our hypocrisy. Our conscience is constantly and necessarily squashed. This emptiness and guilt over our misrepresenting of the truth is a massive weight. Then add the fear of the other person finding out. I have seen the huge relief after a person has come clean confirming it through the use of a polygraph. Come clean and enjoy the freedom from the weight of your lies and your two-facedness in life.

- **To Break Down Walls of Isolation.** Manipulating a person makes us feel shallow. We know we are hurting them so we pull back from those we lie to. Through maintaining relational distance for fear of discovery, we cannot help but withholding closeness. Whether before marriage of after, the connection is superficial at best. We cannot be spinning lies to our spouse and be growing closer. We know our undisclosed life – those untrue words and actions – would hurt them so we deliberately keep our distance emotionally.

- **To Destroy the Enemy's Foothold.** Satan clearly gets a foothold in our life through the relational breakdowns caused by lying and anger (Ephesians 4: 25-27). Seriously, his power over us grows in the secrets we keep. Break the silence to break the power and fully come clean. Don't believe his lies that you can get away with it – that you won't get caught. You will. Your ongoing misrepresenting of the truth is destroying you and your most important relationships.

When Should I Come Clean

Sooner than later and the sooner, the better. When asked by a person trapped in an extra-marital affair, "Should I tell my wife (or husband)?" My usual response is, "What time today should we meet to tell them?" I so deeply believe that a person is foolish to push against God's clear design for honesty in relationships. Come clean. Honor God. Remove the wedge. Begin the changes needed. Begin the healing.

How Should I Come Clean

1. **Set Up a Time to Come Clean.** Be sure that you both have a significant amount of time alone together to work through the initial hurt and painful reactions. Don't choose to disclose just before one of you is leaving to be somewhere else. Respect the need for process time.

2. **Initiate the Confession.** Choose to come clean before getting caught. Disclosure is far better than discovery. Take the first step of integrity by volunteering your mistakes and your lies. Don't leave your spouse wondering if your behavior would still be going on if it hadn't been discovered.

3. **Admit Your Wrongs.** Own your sin and selfishness. Disclose all secret behavior. Start speaking truthfully. No more half-truths. No minimizing. No explaining, justifying or clarifying. Excuses are to be avoided. Face your wrongs openly. I am so committed to helping people to come clean with full disclosure that I use polygraphs in my counseling practice to confirm the truth.

4. **Avoid Progressive Disclosure.** Don't believe that not telling the person everything will be better. Don't slowly tell more of the story to see how they will take it. Those confessing often only share part of their failure as if it is all of it. They sometimes even say, "No, that's everything," only to admit more of the story in the days ahead. Progressive Disclosure is a relational killer! A half-hearted or incomplete attempt to come clean will cause greater damage, doubt and pain. Remember: Come fully clean.

5. **Apologize with Sincerity.** Confess your failures. Own your mistakes. Start your journey toward looking at life through your spouse's eyes. It will not be easy to show empathy toward the pain you have caused. Your selfishness is so deep. Apologize fully for your failure and betrayal. Ask for forgiveness giving them time to process where they are at in their journey of betrayal recovery.

6. **Surrender Your Digital World.** Come clean online too by giving all your passwords to your devices and your social interaction programs – all forms of instant messaging and emailing. Better still – get off all social media! Give them full access to your phone and any other devices as part of your coming clean.

7. **Cut Off Access to the Distraction.** Whether it's an affair, hiding spending, porn use or other moral or relational failures, completely block all opportunity for ongoing temptation to continue with the inappropriate behavior. Talk out a viable game plan to cut off all access to troublesome temptations.

8. **Be Willing to Be Accountable.** Volunteer your actions, your schedule and your whereabouts. Check in often. Answer all questions openly and honestly. Take calls. Account for all your time willingly. Agree to be accountable to someone beyond your spouse. Find someone your spouse trusts – someone with "teeth". Telling the truth needs to be your mandate moving forward. Fight the habit of withholding. Speak the truth, period!

9. **Seek Outside Help.** To rebuild after a difficult disclosure may be rather hard. Often it is wise to have a pastor or counselor mediate initially and guide you in the rebuilding of trust. An objective and caring sounding board for the hurting partner is usually best if the betrayal has been significant. Make sure your spouse has ready access to godly, caring support through the disclosure. It won't come from you.

10. **Reconnect Spiritually.** Take the steps to get your life on track. Go to God for His forgiveness and strength to live right. Get back to church to have your faith reinforced. Seek the Lord daily in prayer and Bible reading to anchor your recovery.

James 5:16 may be the best summary: "Therefore confess your sins to each other and pray for each other so that you may be healed. The prayer of a righteous person is powerful and effective." Come clean. Live clean. Support others in their desire to be clean. You will never regret the step to start living an authentic life.

DISCUSSION STARTERS:

1. Are you being honest with your partner? Are you withholding things for fear of rejection? Are you carrying shame and guilt for choices made? CHOOSE NOW. Determine to come clean on everything. No secrets. They need to be able to love you for who you are not for who you portray to be.

2. Agree as a couple to follow through on the "Coming Clean" steps given in this chapter.

3. Complete the Sexual History Survey. Agree on a time to share your results honestly and openly – the failures and unfaithfulness – both privately and publicly. Include your pornography use without minimizing or lying about it.

Sexual History Survey

Filled out by: ❏ Husband ❏ Wife   Date: _____

The purpose of this survey is to get to "Ground Zero" in your sexual trust by fostering full disclosure and open discussion between husband and wife on many critical issues in the area of their sexual history. Honesty can bring confidence and freedom that will create a solid foundation for a lasting marriage.

Instructions:
- Answers should refer to your whole life before and after marriage or any spiritual conversion.
- Instructions: Mark an "X" in the appropriate boxes of each of the following statements:
  Never, O – once, R – rarely: 2-3 times or F - frequently: 4 or more times.
- Two boxes per line may be checked if a problem is both past and present. Present refers to the last 6 months.

SCORING   ISSUES OF SEXUAL EXPERIENCE

Never Past Present
        O R F   O R F

❏ ❏❏❏ ❏❏❏ 1. I have been drawn to and watch questionable and sensuous TV dramas and/ or soaps.

❏ ❏❏❏ ❏❏❏ 2. I have stayed up late to watch movies with clear sensuous themes or images.

❏ ❏❏❏ ❏❏❏ 3. I have purchased and/or read magazines that have negative sexual articles.

❏ ❏❏❏ ❏❏❏ 4. I have purchased/read popular novels that have questionable sexual themes.

❏ ❏❏❏ ❏❏❏ 5. I have attended R-rated movies at theaters that shows pornographic material.

❏ ❏❏❏ ❏❏❏ 6. I have attended an "adult" movie theater that shows pornographic material.

❏ ❏❏❏ ❏❏❏ 7. I have rented pornographic movies to view privately at home or with friends.

❏ ❏❏❏ ❏❏❏ 8. I have purchased and/or read pornographic magazines or books.

❏ ❏❏❏ ❏❏❏ 9. I have purchased, rented and/or viewed pornographic videos.

❏ ❏❏❏ ❏❏❏ 10. I have purchased and/or read hard-core or "illegal" pornographic material.

❏ ❏❏❏ ❏❏❏ 11. I have watched pornographic previews and/or channels while staying in hotels.

❏ ❏❏❏ ❏❏❏ 12. I have watched the pornographic channels that I get with a satellite dish.

❏ ❏❏❏ ❏❏❏ 13. I have viewed pornographic previews and/or websites on the Internet.

❏ ❏❏❏ ❏❏❏ 14. I have texted or emailed sexual messages to someone other than my spouse.

❏ ❏❏❏ ❏❏❏ 15. I have previewed or participated in the phone-sex market (state #: _____).

❏ ❏❏❏ ❏❏❏ 16. I have attended and/or participated in the pornographic viewing at peep shows.

❏ ❏❏❏ ❏❏❏ 17. I have attended nightclubs with exotic dancers or strippers.

❏ ❏❏❏ ❏❏❏ 18. I have viewed or distributed child pornography.

❏ ❏❏❏ ❏❏❏ 19. I have participated in the filming of pornographic video footage.

❏ ❏❏❏ ❏❏❏ 20. I have been involved in an all men's/women's party where there was a stripper.

❏ ❏❏❏ ❏❏❏ 21. I have been given to flirting or suggestive teasing with people other than my spouse.

❏ ❏❏❏ ❏❏❏ 22. I have dated two people at one time without the other knowing.

❏ ❏❏❏ ❏❏❏ 23. I have been tempted by or attracted to another person's physical, sexual or personality attributes other than my spouse.

❏ ❏❏❏ ❏❏❏ 24. I have been emotionally bonded to another person other than my spouse since beginning to date him/her.

❏ ❏❏❏ ❏❏❏ 25. I have roaming eyes, repeatedly focusing on the sexual part of female/male body.

❏ ❏❏❏ ❏❏❏ 26. I have sought out old flames on Facebook without my spouse's awareness.

❏ ❏❏❏ ❏❏❏ 27. I have attended nightclubs in order to pick up a girl or guy.

❏ ❏❏❏ ❏❏❏ 28. I have been involved in same sex mutual masturbation experiences.

❏ ❏❏❏ ❏❏❏ 29. I have had pre-marital sexual involvement as an adult with someone other than my spouse (state #: _____).

❏ ❏❏❏ ❏❏❏ 30. I have masturbated or practiced other types of sexual self-stimulation.

❏ ❏❏❏ ❏❏❏ 31. I have struggled with the issue of persistent or habitual masturbation.

❏ ❏❏❏ ❏❏❏ 32. I have engaged in online sexual encounters with live audio or video contact.

❏ ❏❏❏ ❏❏❏ 33. I was sexually active as a teenager.

❏ ❏❏❏ ❏❏❏ 34. I have had pre-marital sexual involvement with my spouse (state #: _____).

❏ ❏❏❏ ❏❏❏ 35. I have used the date rape drug or got dates drunk to take advantage of them.

❏ ❏❏❏ ❏❏❏ 36. I have been involved in oral sex prior to marriage.

❏ ❏❏❏ ❏❏❏ 37. I have been involved in anal sex prior to marriage.

❏ ❏❏❏ ❏❏❏ 38. I have had sexual intercourse with someone other than my spouse (state #: _____).

❏ ❏❏❏ ❏❏❏ 39. I have had sex with someone for money, drugs or favors.

❏ ❏❏❏ ❏❏❏ 40. I have called and been involved with a person from an escort service (state #: _____).

❏ ❏❏❏ ❏❏❏ 41. I have been involved in a sexual affair since I've been dating my spouse.

❏ ❏❏❏ ❏❏❏ 42. I have aggressively pressured a man/woman beyond their point of comfort in sexual involvement (state #: _____).

❏ ❏❏❏ ❏❏❏ 43, I have gone to an adult massage parlor (state #: _____).

❏ ❏❏❏ ❏❏❏ 44. I have been sexually involved with a prostitute (state #: _____).

❏ ❏❏❏ ❏❏❏ 45. I have forcibly raped a date, girl/boyfriend, acquaintance or stranger.

❏ ❏❏❏ ❏❏❏ 46. I have forcibly raped my spouse.

❏ ❏❏❏ ❏❏❏ 47. I have been raped by a date, girl/boyfriend, acquaintance, or stranger.

❏ ❏❏❏ ❏❏❏ 48. I have been raped by my spouse.

❏ ❏❏❏ ❏❏❏ 49. I have reason to fear that my sexual history yields a clear possibility of AIDS.

❏ ❏❏❏ ❏❏❏ 50. I have been involved in a cross-dressing experience that had a sexual purpose.

❏ ❏❏❏ ❏❏❏ 51. I have been involved in sexual touching experience as a child with other children.

❏ ❏❏❏ ❏❏❏ 52. I have been involved in a threesome – more than two people in sexual activity.

❏ ❏❏❏ ❏❏❏ 53. I am given to violence wrongly associated with sexual involvement.

❏ ❏❏❏ ❏❏❏ 54. I have willingly been involved in a homosexual experience (state #: _____).

❏ ❏❏❏ ❏❏❏ 55. I have touched children in an inappropriate sexual way.

❏ ❏❏❏ ❏❏❏ 56. I have touched my own children in an inappropriate sexual way.

❏ ❏❏❏ ❏❏❏ 57. I was sexually abused as a child or young teen by an adult.

❏ ❏❏❏ ❏❏❏ 58. I was sexually abused as a child or young teen by an adult of the same sex.

❏ ❏❏❏ ❏❏❏ 59. I have been involved in occultic or ritualistic sexual experiences.

❏ ❏❏❏ ❏❏❏ 60. I have had sex with an animal.

❏Yes ❏ No 61. I have a secret sexual life no one knows about; the details are on the back.

❏Yes ❏ No 62. I have taken steps to deal with my sexual struggles by reaching out to others.

❏Yes ❏ No 63. I am fully satisfied with the sexual relationship with my spouse in our marriage.

❏Yes ❏ No 64. I have talked openly to my spouse about all of these issues.

❏Yes ❏ No 65. I fear my spouse rejecting me over my private or past sexual experiences.

Chapter 13
Are You a Student of Your Spouse?
Discover Your Differences
Jody Wandzura

As part of our Master's degrees in Educational Leadership, my husband and I did our final project on Relationship Education for Middle School Students, High School Students and Engaged Couples. We researched and evaluated over forty different premarital counseling, relationship education, and marriage resources.

We were so focused on getting our major project done that we didn't realize how much it would test our relationship. If you had been a fly on the wall in our house, you would have laughed as we struggled to write this 268-page paper together. We stopped talking while writing the communication section. We fought during the conflict resolution chapter. I held a grudge when he did not complete the forgiveness chapter on time. We stopped going on dates because we were too busy researching the friendship section. It was a completely humbling experience! It made us realize how much we still needed to learn and grow!

We can laugh *now* when we think of all the grief it caused our marriage, but it took some time to realize what had happened. While we struggled under the stress of completion dates, in the end, we learned many things about marriage, especially about each other. For us, the most significant takeaway was to humbly keep being a student of your spouse. Ask the questions, "Who are you? How do you like to be treated? And what makes you feel loved?"

Who Are You?
Understanding Personality

God has created each person to be unique. You are born into your family with a personality. Just think about your brother or your sister. Are you different or the same as them? Do you respond to life the way they do? Are you interested in the same things? In my family, I am the oldest of four somewhat different kids. I am energetic, passionate and competitive; my brother, born next, is mentally tough, hard-working and calm; my sister is creative, bubbly and empathetic; my youngest brother is patient, trustworthy and thoughtful. Same parents. Same family. Same upbringing. Different kids.

Personality is who God made you to be and is part of who you are. Your disposition does not generally change over your life, but many influences can shape who you are – positive and negative. These influences can include people in your world, abilities, successes, failures, physical traits, and cultural influences. You may not have known your spouse for long, so it is essential to learn how their past shaped who they are today.

Take some time to have fun interacting on these topics. Ask each other the following questions to further discover your differences.

1. Personality: List six words that describe your personality. What personality strengths do you see in yourself? What are some common weaknesses to do with your character?

2. Family of Origin: Describe what it was like growing up in your family. How have they shaped your worldview?

3. Physical Traits: Growing up where you lived, how did your physical appearance or abilities impact who you are today? (size, ethnicity, athleticism etc.)

4. Influences: Who were the major influencers in your life? Who had the most positive impact on your life? Who was the most negative?

5. Energy: What energizes you or fills you up? What depletes you of joy? How do you recharge? What do you need to stay balanced?

6. Compatibility: What do you look for in friendship? What kind of people do you enjoy being with? Who brings you life? What type of person rubs you the wrong way?

7. Conflict: What happens to you when a problem comes up? Do you down play or deny issues? Describe how you handle conflict, including confronting, apologizing, forgiving and releasing.

8. Stress: What kinds of things stress you out? What kinds of things do I do to cause stress? How does your behavior change if you become stressed?

9. Success/Failure: What are some of the biggest successes in your life? What are some of your biggest failures? How do you feel about these now?

10. Confidence: What is your level of self-confidence out of 10? What do you struggle with about yourself? What has led to these feelings?

How Do You Like to Be Treated?
The Difference Between Male and Female Preferences

When trying to understand your spouse, it helps to learn how males and females differ. I read many books on this topic in our research, but too often, the books contradict or contain information I disagreed with. To simplify the differences between males and females in marriage, I created the WOW vs. WOO factors. Men want the WOW, and women want the WOO.

WOW Your Man: Most men desire to overcome and receive recognition as a champion in life. Even more important, men want to be respected to feel loved. A man needs to provide for his wife and family. He wants to succeed at work and overcome challenges. He wants to feel admired and to have his woman pursue him sexually. He desires to be a good father and a good husband. Most of all, he appreciates recognition for trying to do all these things.

If you want to give your man all he needs, it all comes down to applying the WOW factor. When you look at your guy, do you adore him and respect him for who he is, what he does, his opinions, his thoughts and his companionship? What do your eyes say when you look at him? What do your words portray when you speak to him? Men want to hear WOW and be admired and respected – it will help them become the men they want to be.

It is like a story I once heard: A mayor and his wife pulled up to a gas station, and they noticed the man working there was a past boyfriend of the wife. The mayor smugly stated, "Aren't you glad you married the mayor?" To which the wife replied, "If I had married him, he would be the mayor!"

Do you WOW your man into being the best version of himself?

WOO Your Woman: Conversely, women want to feel desirable, beautiful and loved. Women need to know their opinions and feelings are heard and respected. The WOO factor means pursuing her, serving her, wanting to spend time with her, romancing her and showing her that she is genuinely loved. It asks the man to connect in a friendship by listening to each other and sharing thoughts, feelings and struggles. It is taking the time to apologize and reconcile.

When dating, a man will look deep into her eyes, confirming that she is the only one he notices. He will create ways to make her feel treasured and valued. But sometimes, men stop WOOing their woman after the altar. They say, "I did it! I've won her over! She's mine." Then, they quit doing the things a woman needs throughout the marriage.

When you continue to WOO her, she will flourish and grow in ways you could not have imagined. Interestingly enough, your WOO leads to her WOW!

What Makes You Feel Loved?
Understanding Expressions of Love

Three simple ways to express love are speaking, doing and giving. It is essential to practice all three to demonstrate love fully.

Speaking

Words are so powerful. They can build up or tear down, so we must choose them carefully. Make your words encouraging and supportive. Share these words with your spouse – especially when others are around! You can even write uplifting words on a card for them to read. Choose words of love.

My dad is a words guy. He feels loved when people take the time to write him a note and encourage him. He also appreciates when people publicly praise him for who he is and what he does. Although most people appreciate encouragement, it means more to some.

Doing

You can show your mate love by doing things *with* them and *for* them. "With them" is spending time together, like going on dates or being alone. "For them" refers to something you do that benefits them, like washing their car or making a romantic dinner.

My husband and I both appreciate the expression of Doing. We love spending time together. We enjoy biking, board games, playing badminton, rollerblading, going for dinner and watching movies together. At the same time, I especially like doing things for Chris to serve him. When I want to show him love, I refold all his shirts in the closet or make a meal for him. I feel so thankful when he cleans our kitchen, replaces light bulbs, or goes grocery shopping. We are definitely do-ers!

Giving

Giving can be in the form of material gifts or physical attention. A gift does not have to be expensive but requires thought and selflessness. Consider a flower picked in a field or a smoothie grabbed on the way home from work. A little gift says, "I thought of you and love you." You can also give the gift of physical attention; it could be shown through eye contact, sitting close, holding hands, or a long hug. This type of expression says, "you are the only one for me."

So, it is time to go back to school and study your spouse! Be a student by learning more about who they are, how they like to be treated and what makes them feel loved.

DISCUSSION STARTERS:

1. PERSONALITY DIFFERENCES: Once you have completed the ten categories, what is one thing you learned about your spouse's background and personality? How has this helped you understand them better?

2. GENDER DIFFERENCES: What did you learn about the differences between men and women? In what ways could each of you do a better job demonstrating WOO or WOW? Share one suggestion for how your spouse could improve.

3. EXPRESSING LOVE DIFFERENCES: List one idea in each option of speaking, doing and giving to demonstrate love this week to each other. Which option means the most to you?

Chapter 14
Digital Delirium:
Are Electronic Devices Anti-Marriage?
Dr. Dave Currie

Between my cellphone, iPad and laptop, digital technology has made my life better. I can do life faster and more efficiently. I depend on it daily. I rely on it deeply. I am seriously bent out of shape if one of my devices is not cooperating. Convenience to life – yes. Enhancement to life – yes. Permanence to life – yes.

But is there more? What is the overall impact of our culture's digital delirium? Are there any negative effects on our most important relationships? It appears so.

In the last year in my private practice, I have had three couples come desperately needing help to create *Digital Boundaries* for their marriage. Each felt that their spouse's cellphone attachment for any and every reason was causing mounting and damaging stress between them. I am convinced that what these couples have recognized is just the tip of the iceberg. I believe the impact of device addiction on the current version of marriage is deeply significant. Here's what I am seeing as some of the effects of digital imbalance.

Damaging Distractions in the Present

- **Skewed priorities develop**. Activities and people that were once central to our world are set aside for a new loyalty and preoccupation to the digital flavour of the month. Whether it's a new app or a well-worn standard one, the attraction repeatedly lures us off to our technological mistress and away from building genuine ties with our mate.

- **Significant time wasted.** You won't likely want to try this, but why not monitor your use of digital devices for one week? For iPhones, it's called Screen Time. Turn it on. It measures every app you use. The clock doesn't lie. Where are your minutes and hours slipping away? Facebook, Clash of Clans, Snapchat, YouTube, interacting or gaming of any kind – look at the time spent with your face in the screen. Interesting how you can fritter away ten to twelve hours a week online (a kind estimate for some) but not have time for a date with your spouse.

- **Social boundaries blur.** I'm not sure of all the reasons why but it appears that people will say and do things through a text or a video that they would never say or do in person. Values fade and relational limits seem to get distorted. Perhaps this compromise happens because we think we are not hurting anyone, that nobody will know, that it's just a joke or innocent fun. Flirting with others, sexual talk, dirty jokes, taking dares, sharing intimate information, exchanging questionable photos and more can draw us inadvertently closer to another person other than our mate.

- **Secrets are stored.** What are you hiding? Are there things on your phone you don't want your spouse to see like photos, chats or connections with people that would damage your primary relationship. Are you erasing your search history? Are you finding yourself guarding your phone like a dog on a bone? Do you withhold passwords and get furious feeling your privacy is being invaded if they ask? Enough said. You are out of line. Relational confusion and its power over you grow in secret.

- **Selfishness unleashed.** Do you watch or read material that is destructive to your marriage? Do you erase your search history to hide what's going on? Do you actually pursue relationships online without your spouse's knowledge? Dating sites? Chat rooms? Discreet affair sites? Are you hooked on pornography? The online world can feed deep and dark pastimes and lead you to pull away further from your spouse.

I believe this is just the beginning for sorrows. How will all this technology impact the future of our most important relationships? Some may call my projections speculation but I may be one of the more experienced family experts to be able to prognosticate the extent of the digital distance forthcoming in marriage. Frankly, it seems to be happening already.

Developing Dysfunction in the Future

With a growing attachment to our various devices as our primary means of interaction, here's what I believe is on the relational, and thus, marital horizon.

- **Misunderstandings will increase.** Less and less communication will be face-to-face and more misinterpretations, stresses and fights will result. Remember, when addressing heart issues or hard feelings, only 7% of our communication is expressed by our words with 38% attributed to our tone or attitude and 55% is body language (www.masterclass.com, 2020). We really miss a ton when we only text or email. With no eye contact, no sense of their heart or intent and no way to read congruence of the body, we really are guessing as to the true meaning of the instant message. The text version of the story, much shorter than the Reader's Digest version, just can't be as clear. And no, emojis or emoticons are not enough.

- **Patience will be a lost virtue.** The term, *instant messaging* says it all. We want to know now! We want answers now! We want a response NOW! Why aren't they answering? What's more important? What are they avoiding? Friction will literally grow by the minute when we get no response. We will continue to grow this immediate need to resolve things fast. Our relational exasperation through impatience could poison many a good relationship. This is never good for resolving conflicts.

- **Deep conversations will fade.** With a strict budget on communication, most will struggle with the longer interactions in person that build close connection. Real social skills will be lacking. There will be less and less actual "face time". Initially, we will be pushing the "get to the point" approach, but in reality, we will not have learned how to settle in, really listen and engage in actual conversations. Long talks in person will become less and less the norm. Relational shallowness will pervade.

- **_Restraint will dwindle._** People will continue to grow more bravado in speaking their mind through texts and emails. In reactionary moments, pushing send with an angry response is much like saying "so there"! We somehow feel more confident to say it like it is when the person isn't in the room. But remember, hurtful written statements become a permanent record and can be saved and brooded over for decades – every word, every sentence reviewed to deepen the resentment. And a discretion monitor for our lips is much more likely to be found than a filter on our fingertips. Keys will spew venom more easily and more frequently.

So, what's a wise, technologically savvy person supposed to do? Can you be relationally close to your spouse if you are digitally addicted? Stay tuned for Chapter 15 - **Finding Wise Digital Boundaries.**

DISCUSSION STARTERS:

1. Honestly admit: how big a problem is your device addiction? Score each other out of 10 with 10 meaning a massive distraction and 1 meaning little to no distraction.

   HIM -   /10   HER-   /10

2. State your opinion on your relational-digital balance as a couple. How balanced are you?

3. List two things that bother you the most regarding your devices and their challenge to your relationship:
   -
   -

4. Agree to turn on and monitor both of your Screen Times or equivalent in an android. Discuss if there's a need for setting limits.

Chapter 15
Finding Wise Digital Boundaries

Dr. Dave Currie

Unchecked digital habits are sucking the life out of too many marriages. I'm talking about all the time, energy and attention that goes to everything "screen time": Facebook, texting, emailing, surfing, YouTube, Instagram, Snapchat, online gaming, Kindle and a myriad of opportunities, attractions and apps that are increasingly preoccupying our lives and side-tracking our focus. Digital distraction is having a growing tendency toward hampering relational connection. Marriages are suffering.

The following bit of news might sound crazy but it screams my point! The word *"Facebook"* is now appearing in the courtroom records in just over 20% of the divorce cases in Great Britain. We know that North America is even likely more cellphone saturated. In some ways, the monthly explosion of new devices and apps to 'make our lives better' is nearing the destructive impact of a full on 'Digital Desert Storm' assault on your most important relationships. Making our lives better – yah, right!

So, to the point: The Why and How of Wise Digital Boundaries.

Why Create Digital Boundaries for Your Marriage?

Face it, two's company but three's a crowd even when the third person is your PHONE. The goal needs to be finding more "US" time as a couple – time to walk, talk, interact and connect. Time alone. Too many couples fight to consistently carve out even a little time to date. It is hard but when both the date nights and the shorter daily interactions are cut up by the interruption of others (the phone calls, texts and notifications), there is less and less alone and connection time.

For some, the delirium is in addictive proportions. They almost panic without the phone in hand like a digital junkie in need of a fix.

Turn the phone off. Put it away. Leave it in the car. Why?

Undivided attention screams validation.

You are saying to your spouse, "You are more important than all others. I am fully here with you". Donalyn has asked me from time to time when we are heading out on a date (and yes, we need to do that too), "Who's coming with us?" What she is humorously reminding me that if my phone is along, so are the 4700+ contacts that are in my phone. Any of which could be the one to interrupt us – so in essence, 4700 are coming with us if I don't turn the phone off, leave it in the car or turn on the do not disturb.

So, like us, with the phone or other devices in play, you are never alone. You are not locked into the live face-to-face interaction with your spouse. You are not content in the moment. You are not fully present. Further, another person's text brings their presence – they are now in the room with you because they are now on your mind. You let them interrupt your time with your spouse. So, to your mate, something or someone else is the priority.

And with the repeated interruptions, it's hard to settle into deeper face-to-face interactions because of the broken flow of conversation. You just don't go as deep or as personal. Both can be a challenge to any marriage.

Why not take a page out of Donalyn's book and use these questions to guide you:
- ARE WE ALONE?
- IS SOMEONE JOINING US?
- WHO ELSE IS COMING?
- ARE YOU BRINGING SOMEONE WITH US?

Pick one and make it your catch phrase as a couple to declare war on the digital distractions.

How to Set Practical Digital Boundaries to Strengthen Your Marriage

You are not the only couple needing help here. I just worked through specific digital boundaries with another couple just last week (fourth in the last year or so). Many couples are finding the electronic distractions a serious challenge to their relationship. It's the growing number of couples coming for help in this area that prompted me to write this for all marriages to benefit. I'll actually be sharing some of the ideas here that I shared with them in my office.

Here's a list of possible digital guidelines. I suggest you read and discuss them with your spouse. Agree on the ones you will try to implement for the next three months to limit the screen time distractions and create a better connection between you. Then evaluate and make the improvements needed.

HOT TIP: Listen to our DFR Podcast #71: **Technology's Attack on Marriage – Finding Wise Digital Boundaries** to hear more on this discussion you've just read about.

1. No electronics including calls, texts and TV during meal times. Lock in on each other for at least twenty minutes. Music is okay.

2. No entertainment or social electronics until your evening work or chores related to family are done. Put the phones away until the evening tasks are complete.

3. No electronics before spending quality time with family and helping with the evening routine. Work to be present with the family and not always reaching for your phone.

4. No electronics while a family member wants to discuss a concern or problem. Put it out of reach.

5. Limit digital distractions while on dates or try to shut them down completely.

6. No electronics in bed or any digital contact with others in the bedroom. Don't sit in bed scrolling, surfing, messaging, commenting and the like. Go to bed holding only one thing – your sweetheart.

7. Work to go to bed together at least five times each week. Late nights alone on the computer or phone surfing, gaming, or browsing needs to be limited.

8. Move the TV out of the bedroom for six months and see if it makes a difference to your connection.

9. No electronics while your mate is driving. Be in the moment WITH your spouse trying to engage warmly. Be available to interact as much as possible. Let driving time be "Us" time.

10. Don't let TV be your default activity together as a couple more than two nights/week.

11. If you know you are expecting an important work-related call during family or couple time, give notice to your spouse or the family.

12. Agree to turn your phones or other devices off for one hour every evening.

13. What other guidelines do you feel are needed to help draw you closer as a couple?

NOTE: Your goal is to create and then these digital boundaries is to make "US" a priority again with ample face-to-face time and great treatment of each other. May God help you put your marriage and family first.

DISCUSSION STARTERS:

1. Discuss the current level of digital distraction in your marriage. Will you agree to work together to try to do something about it? It is possible that one of you is more challenged in this area than your spouse. Will you bravely look at adjustments that could and should be made?

   Yes, I am all in to create wise digital boundaries for our marriage. _____

   No, I don't think we need or I want digital boundaries for our marriage. _____

2. To create your marital digital boundaries, discuss the 13 suggestions above and either adjust, accept or omit the guideline.

3. Put your final list on paper and actually post it in the kitchen and the bedroom. Keep a copy of it on your phone. It's okay if the kid's serve as device police. Try it for three months, then discuss boundaries and evaluate how the changes have affected your marriage.

Chapter 16
Clear Speech:

Understanding the Communication Package

Jody Wandzura

Take a moment to think of all the current forms of communication: Facebook, Zoom, iMessage, email, texting, Snapchat, Instagram, WhatsApp, FaceTime and even the old-fashioned face-to-face chat at a coffee shop. Communication is everywhere and is consistently presenting itself in many new formats. While our methods are expanding, I often wonder if our communication ability is shrinking!

Relational communication is a crucial component of any marriage. It is "the process by which people exchange information, feelings, and meaning through verbal and non-verbal messages to develop and maintain a healthy relationship" (www.skillsyouneed.com, 2020). This interpersonal exchange may be just a simple message between two people, but it is so much more intricate than it sounds.

There are three significant variables that can influence a message: the actual words used, the tone of one's voice and the body language displayed. Sociological research has shown that when sharing emotions with someone, any message that's loaded with feeling, these three aspects of interaction display an interesting mix. While not relevant to matters of mere information or facts, take a guess further at the percentage of each aspect when expressing feeling.

Words are _____% of the whole message.
Tone is _____% of the whole message.
Body Language is _____% of the whole message.
Total message: 100%

Once your final guesses are in, read on!

WORDS

When expressing matters of the heart, the breakdown of the three aspects is: words create only 7%, the tone is 38%, and body language is 55%. (www.masterclass.com, 2020). The first time I heard this stat, I was surprised at how little the words impacted the message compared to tone and body language. It reminds me of my high school volleyball teammate who confronted me, saying, "I know you are saying "good job" with your words, but *how* you say it feels the opposite." For the record, she was right: my tone did not match my words. My tone conveyed how I really felt frustrated with her.

Regardless of their overall power, words still have the potential to either build up or tear down, so we must choose our words carefully. Proverbs 12:18 says, "the words of the reckless pierce like swords, but the tongue of the wise brings healing." Do your actual words build up your spouse, or are they slowly stabbing holes in them? I have been guilty of jabbing comments more often than I would care to admit.

To prevent careless and hurtful words, we need to run our thoughts through the THNK filter to see if they pass the test before we speak. The THNK acrostic is helpful in all areas of life with all people. Here are four questions to consider:
1. **T – Is it true?** Do I know that everything I am about to speak is from a trustworthy source and is entirely true?
2. **H – Is it helpful?** Does my message aim to build up the other person and genuinely help them in life? Or might it be gossip and, therefore, unhelpful?
3. **N – Is it necessary?** Do I need to say this, or should I just let it go?
4. **K – Is it kind?** Is my message kind and motivated by love?

I recently used the THNK filter as I was frustrated with my husband and wanted to let him know. I felt irritated that he often left a pile of shoes at the bottom of the stairs, so before I approached him, here is what the process sounded like.

First of all, is my message true? Yes, he leaves the shoes there. Often.

Secondly, is my message helpful? Maybe not. He leaves them there because he usually carries many things in his arms while in the middle of home improvement projects. He also does not like to bring his muddy shoes into the house. Hmm. Those are all good reasons. If I asked him to focus on his shoes, he may do fewer home improvements. Besides, putting all his shoes away would only take me thirty seconds.

Thirdly, is it necessary that I speak to him? I must say *something* because I often trip on the shoes and feel frustrated that I might roll my ankle. Plus, he has four shelves of shoe space available; he just needs to get them there.

Finally, is it kind and out of love? Maybe. Timing is essential to demonstrate kindness. After thinking it through, I think the best opportunity would be when we are already in the garage and I see him taking off his shoes. I would explain to him that I am worried about tripping and hurting myself. Saying it like this would come across with kindness.

What type of topics could you use the THNK filter: the new haircut, helping around the house, bad habits, or certain meals? However, what if the topic of discussion is higher in intensity? His addiction, her weight, his parents, or her spending habits. These types of discussions also need to be thoroughly planned using the chapters on conflict resolution and could require advice or assistance from a professional counselor.

TONE
The tone part of the message, which accounts for a large portion of the meaning, is the emotion coming out in sound: angry, sad, joyful, disgusted, scared, thrilled, tired, frustrated, interested, peaceful, confused, annoyed, amused, sarcastic, bothered and so on. The tone you choose while conveying your feelings determines the meaning of the words. Sometimes you don't choose; your tone is just there!

You can merely make a sound and convey a message without saying a word. Think about a satisfied sigh: "Ahhhhhhhh." Or a frustrated huff: "Ahh!" Or the high-pitched squeal I make while clapping when I see a friend I have not seen in a long time: "AAAAHHHHH!" Or even the kung-fu noise I make when I drop an egg on the floor: "Deahhhhhhh!" While these noises have similar letters, the tone and subsequent meaning are drastically different!

When my husband and I disagree, he often feels like I am attacking him. Usually, I have little emotion attached to what I am saying, but I speak too "passionately." We have figured out that my tone is intense, strong, and maybe too rushed. I now see this in my kids' responses, helping me realize what my husband means. I have often told my kids, "What you are saying may be correct, but how you say it is not making our home a better place to live in!" I am trying to take my own advice. Daily.

BODY LANGUAGE

Body language contains the most significant part in communicating your feelings. Body language includes facial expressions, body posture, arm actions, proximal distance, eye contact, and touch.

Even young children read body language. When my son was only four, I took him and a buddy to a children's indoor play center. I watched from a distance as a third boy approached them and crawled up on the jeep. My son saw his friend and the new boy having fun and attempted to climb up, too. This new boy said nothing, but his body language told the whole story. I witnessed a scowling face and a straight arm with his palm facing out. My son disregarded the first signs of rejection, but once he was up, that boy put his back to him, blocking him from coming in.

Moments later, my son returned to me with a quivering lip. I saw everything I needed to understand his feelings, but I wanted him to discuss them. He sadly reported, "That boy said he does not want to play with me." I inquired deeper: "Did you *hear* him say those words?" He thought for a moment, and with tear-brimming eyes looking right into mine, he sighed. "No...but that is what he was saying." No words. No tone. But a clear message.

MIXED MESSAGES

When one of the three parts of communication does not match the others, mixed messages occur. Have you ever been part of a miscommunicated conversation? I remember this one time when I was nine months pregnant with my son and feeling enormous! It was a hot summer day, and after grocery shopping, I was returning my cart from the parking lot. A man looked at me and said, straight-faced, "You got a watermelon under there?" How dare he comment on how huge I was! I was fuming! As I pushed my cart back to the storage rack, a fleck of green caught my eye; I had forgotten to unload my watermelon from under my cart! I just laughed! This miscommunication was due to a lack of body language, as he did not motion toward the forgotten melon under the cart.

In the early years of my marriage with Chris, I could have earned the title "Queen of Mixed Messages." Once, we were driving in the car after a minor dispute in which I was "miffed" about something that Chris had said. Being more peace-loving, he asked me, "Is anything wrong?" I snapped back, "I am *fine*" (while looking out the window with my arms crossed, teeth clenched, and my face expressionless). The words insisted that I was okay with the situation, but everything about my tone and body language told another story. I had created a conflicting mixed message and had a perplexed husband.

Becoming a strong communicator takes time and practice. Once you have decided on the message you want to send, make sure you THNK before you speak, select the best tone for your message, and support what you are saying with helpful body language.

DISCUSSION QUESTIONS:

1. What aspect of communication do you struggle with the most? Discuss...
   a. Choosing the right words
   b. Expressing the proper tone in the message
   c. Matching your intended message with your body language

2. Are you guilty of mixed messages? How?

3. What recent miscommunication did you have with your spouse, and how did you work through it? Describe how you could have avoided the miscommunication in the first place.

Chapter 17
Interlocking Lives:
Braiding God Into Your Marriage
Jody Wandzura

I remember, as a six-year-old, my grandmother taught me how to braid. She took three pieces of stretchy fabric and cut them into strips. The strips were all shades of green that made a beautiful pattern when woven together. She also showed me how each strand was pliable and weak but became incredibly strong once braided into a single cord. As a young child, I tried to simplify things and only used two strands, but they quickly unraveled, and my attempts at braiding failed. My grandmother taught me that day that a cord of three strands is the strongest and has the best chance of lasting under tension.

Keep in mind two people in a marriage when you read the following insight:

"Two people are better off than one, for they can help each other succeed. If one person falls, the other can reach out and help. But someone who falls alone is in real trouble. Likewise, two people lying close together can keep each other warm. But how can one be warm alone? A person standing alone can be attacked and defeated, but two can stand back-to-back and conquer. Three are even better, for a triple-braided cord is not easily broken."
(King Solomon – relational wisdom from 950 BC found in Ecclesiastes 4: 9-12, NLT)

When a couple commits their lives to each other, they can choose to braid God in as the third and stabilizing strand. He is the one that will keep them strong individually and together in marriage.

I love the picture – in a braid-like fashion, God wraps Himself around the husband – then He wraps Himself around the wife; then He wraps Himself around the husband – then He wraps Himself around the wife, and so on and so on. He secures them individually and then provides the strength to bind them together – wrapping His arms around them.

In Chapter 11 on intimacy, we talk about the importance of praying together. A couple who prays together stays together! Again, in a study done in 2010 by Christopher Ellison for the *Journal of Marriage and Family*, the statistic was that less than 1% of couples who pray together get divorced. In a world where the divorce is much higher than we would like it, that 1% promise is so reassuring! When God is in the relationship, He binds a couple together and keeps the braid tight and secure.

God

Husband   Wife

Braiding God in really seems to work. This triangle of love diagram shows the importance of including God. As a husband and wife grow closer to God, they also are able to grow closer to each other. Why is this true? Jesus has commanded, "If you love me, keep my commands" (John 14:15), so the Bible is clear that we need to obey God if we love God. As we trust and follow Him, we will grow closer to Him. God says to be kind and patient. God says to say sorry and forgive quickly. God commands us to put others in front of ourselves. If I live my life as God intends, I will become a more delightful person to be around and create a better chance of having a great marriage. That's braiding God in.

There are many ways for a couple to strengthen their cord of three and ultimately grow in their relationship with God. Let's look at how to braid God in: learn together, serve together and connect together.

LEARNING TOGETHER

One of the easiest ways to strengthen your cord is to learn together. This is what you are doing right now! Learning about God's perspective on marriage and sharing your thoughts will help you grow! There are countless books, podcasts and articles that you can learn from and then discuss.

There are also courses and groups you can join. My husband and I have attended a group study called Alpha. It is a great course that teaches foundational principles for having a relationship with God. Even though my husband and I knew the information taught in this course, our group discussion after the lesson was impacting, encouraging and inspiring. On our drive home, we would discuss what we studied and thank God for the insights we gained from the group. We learned and, therefore, grew as a couple!

There are so many ways to learn together. Whether it is a course, a Bible study, a church retreat, a prayer group, an accountability partner, a podcast or reading a book together, learning about God can be an adventure that draws you closer to each other and Him. With continued learning together, your relationship is less likely to unravel.

SERVING TOGETHER

More than just learning together, we have found that serving together is one of the best ways to allow our lives to have purpose and meaning. We grow spiritually! This aspect requires more effort and planning. Ask yourself, "How can we support others, build community and bless someone in our world?" When your joint focus is outward and not just on yourselves, it is meaningful and brings you closer. An effortless way to get involved is to volunteer together at church, like greeting at the front door, teaching Sunday school, leading a life group or serving at the coffee shop. You can do things to bless others—and do them together!

You can grow beyond the church walls too. One of my special memories of serving together was when my mom planned for our family to help a lady down the street. Due to medical circumstances, she was confined to her home, lived alone and couldn't tend to her yard or house. My husband and I joined my parents and other family members in repairing and repainting the fence, weeding the garden, trimming the shrubs, planting flowers in the flower beds and fixing the house. Wow! It was a full day of hard work, but it was all worth it when we saw her looking out her bedroom window with tears running down her face. We still talk about how special that day was for us.

Chris and I have also led eight mission trips with teenagers together. Each trip challenged us to grow in our faith and gave us priceless memories that impacted our students and ourselves. In a recent summer, we took our children to Uganda for three weeks. With the kids' help, we ran a soccer camp for fifty boys and organized sports days for the children of the neighboring village. We visited schools in Uganda and Tanzania, where we did drama, shared testimonies and spent time with the children from the schools. It was a life-changing trip because we could serve together as a family. We have also gone on two family mission trips to Mexico.

Depending on the stage of life and family you are currently in, there are different things you can do to serve and bless others. Before we had kids, we made meals for struggling families, hosted dinners for "new to Canada" neighbors, led clothing drives and helped raise money for different initiatives. When our children were young, we baked cookies together and delivered them to various neighbors. As they got older, we hosted baby showers, invited school families for special dinners and held garage sales to support an African school. We served in each event, allowing us to grow our relationship with God and draw closer together. Serving makes your braid stronger.

CONNECTING TOGETHER

In addition to learning and serving together, connecting with others to do life with is essential. First, look for a mentor couple a life stage or two ahead of you and living life in a way you admire. Spend time with them. Have them over for dinner. Play games together. Just be around them, talk to them, ask them questions and glean from what they do and say.

Secondly, connecting with couples of faith in the same life stage as you is also helpful. You can meet these couples in church, from your sports teams or other extra-curricular activities. Your goal is to build lasting relationships. Joining a small group in a church is an excellent way to meet individuals you can grow with over time. Connecting well with others makes your marital braid even stronger.

Remember, a cord of three strands is less likely to unravel. Try to learn, serve and connect with your spouse in your faith journeys as you seek to braid your lives together.

DISCUSSION STARTERS:

1. When did you fully surrender your life to Jesus? What is your story of faith and transformation?

2. Write out seven significant factors – decisions, events, experiences, influences or people – that have shaped your spiritual journey.

-
-
-
-
-
-
-

3. What could you do to learn more about God as a couple? Suggest one thing to try.

4. What could you do to serve God as a couple? Come up with one idea for the next month.

5. Do you feel connected to others who will help you grow your relationship with God and your marriage? Who could you connect with who would likely help you grow spiritually? List some people here:

-
-
-

Chapter 18
Don't Panic:

Conflict Is Quite Normal

Jody Wandzura

On our street in the Lower Mainland in British Columbia, people are friendly, and we all agree it is a great neighborhood to live in. We know most of our neighbors by name and have grown to appreciate each person. Some come for dinner, and others send their kids to play on our driveway. Everyone is smiling and appears to be happy.

However, the more I get to know them, the more I realize that some happy faces are masks for what is happening inside their homes and hearts. More than half of the families on our street consist of second marriages, blended families and single parents. No judgment implied but four of the seven "for sale" houses were sold in the last year due to separation or divorce.

One neighbor came over smiling and said everything was great, but her house was up for sale the next day. When I asked about the sudden sign, I discovered the sad truth: her common-law partner announced their relationship was over. To make matters worse, her divorce papers from her first marriage were mailed to her that same day. I saw the pain, disappointment and shame in her eyes. This relationaldeterioration in my neighborhood has broken my heart and given me more motivation to complete this book!

Most people get married with the expectation that their marriage will be wonderful and that they will be together "until death do us part." Everyone thinks they know how to keep their relationship strong and healthy, but then we see them post the "for sale" sign. What is happening? What is causing the breakdown between "I do" and "It's over!"?

Understanding Conflict: WEEDS Analogy
First, you must know that conflict is a part of all relationships, including marriage. We understand that conflict is "a lack of agreement or harmony" (Merriam-Webster Dictionary), but often we don't consider why conflict occurs.

When you first start dating, your blossoming friendship is beautiful, and there are usually very few disagreements as you are more focused on growing your relationship and cultivating your love. As time passes, conflicts creep in caused by the slow selfish growth of what could be called "me-me weeds." In every relationship, not just marriage, when we stop putting the other person first, we naturally start thinking about ourselves more.

Relationships are like a garden. When my family planted our first one, everyone chose what they wanted to grow. My husband selected carrots. I wanted tomatoes. My son craved blueberries. My daughter picked raspberries. We all enjoyed a growing harvest of delicious produce for the first two seasons. Halfway through the second season, we started noticing the new growth of more raspberry "canes" in every area of our garden. We tried to dig down and cut them off, but we couldn't stop them. They just kept coming! This year, in early spring, we have noticed that they are coming up even in the far corners of the garden. They will ruin our garden at this rate, so we are getting serious about pulling up all the raspberries before it is too late!

Sometime after the wedding, we start to value what *we* want over what the other person wants, and the selfish seedlings take root. We begin to take each other for granted. We subconsciously think that we no longer need to sow into the relationship and cultivate each other's love as it takes too much time, effort and money. Me-me weeds grow. Sprigs of selfishness, pride, and foolishness take over. My needs. My wants. My opinions. My preferences. My comfort. Like our raspberries, soon things are out of control, me-me weeds grow too fast, and conflicts become more frequent.

Handling Conflict: WALLS Analogy

Any two people will have different values, opinions, and preferences, so there are countless possibilities for disagreements. You may have varying ideas on decorating or which restaurant to eat at. You may not see eye-to-eye about finances. You may dislike what he watches on TV or what she spends her free time doing. You may not grieve or process changes the same way. You may need clarification about how involved your parents should be in your lives. There are endless opportunities for conflict.

Differences, on their own, are not enough alone to cause conflict; we now understand that conflict is caused by mixing differences *with* selfishness. The problem is that we are all sinful people who cause conflict, but it must not be feared. How you handle conflict determines whether it will benefit or harm your relationship. Yes! It can even help you have a stronger relationship.

Imagine that each conflict you face is like a concrete block that is dropped squarely between the two of you. Neither of you wanted the disagreement to happen, but both of you feel strongly about your perspective. So there it sits. What will you do? It doesn't disappear but stubbornly stays put if you ignore or fail to remove it. And the next time you quarrel without working through it, another block is dropped on top of the first. Each argument you have is another significant obstruction. If you continue to ignore the growing pile of conflicts stacking between the two of you, it will result in hurt, frustration and isolation. After a while, a virtual wall separates you from the person you chose to love and cherish.

As time passes, you realize that you are being pushed too far apart and need to deal with the wall of problems, but there are so many blocks that you don't know which one to start working with. You pick up one to resolve it, but soon, you have pulled another couple into the discussion simultaneously. Too complicated. Too frustrating. Too many issues. The conflict has caused division and isolation.

Let's start again but adjust the ending. Imagine that each conflict you face is like a concrete block that is dropped squarely between the two of you. Neither of you wanted the disagreement to happen, but both of you feel strongly about your perspective. So there it sits. What will you do? This time, instead of ignoring it, you immediately deal with it as it lands. Once you agree with how you will settle it, you move the block behind you as a reminder of the victory over that disagreement. Each well-managed block can be carefully placed to build a strong wall around you instead of a massive wall between you.

That sounds easy and obvious, but why doesn't it work for everyone? It requires two critical components: character and skill. First of all, you must have the character traits of self-control, selflessness and humility. Self-control holds your tongue, helps you listen before speaking, and doesn't say or do things you regret. Selflessness takes the focus off you and your needs, wants, opinions, and preferences. Humility puts the emphasis back on others and how you can serve them. The only way we can have these character traits is to focus on God and ask Him for His guidance in this area.

Finally, it also requires specific conflict resolution skills, which will be the focus of the Conflict Resolution in Chapter 21. Using the four Fair Fight steps will lead to successful management of each conflict block so you can move it from becoming a wall between you to a wall around you.

DISCUSSION STARTERS:

1. Weeds: Name the last two times you were selfish in your values, opinions or preferences with your spouse. What did it lead to in your relationship?

   -

   -

2. Walls: How well do you and your mate currently resolve conflict? What are your resolution hurdles?

3. List your current conflicts and discuss what could be done with each block.

Chapter 19
The Mystery of Romance

Dr. Dave Currie

There are few things in life that compare with being "in love." Occupying the center focus of another person's universe is an emotional ecstasy as addicting as any drug. It's simply amazing to feel desired, pursued and valued. We want to be loved for who we are. We also love to love with all our hearts. That wonderful feeling of loving and being loved is innate to all of us. God put it there.

Once we have experienced this healthy sense of loving and being loved, we long for it. We learn all we can about love. Instinctively, we begin to play the romance and kindness game with notes, gifts, flowers and more. We learn to turn on the charm when we want to impress someone. We put our best foot forward on every date. We give gestures of affection and lots of attention. We do this because we love them and want them to love us. And it works. That's partly how you ended up together.

And in great marriages, this romance never ends. That's the heart of lasting connection.

But over time in the dating period, when romance starts to feel like a game, it puts a bad taste in people's mouths. Too often, one's charm is deceitful and one's beauty is fleeting. Sound familiar? It should. We often do what it takes to get what we want. That, of course, is relational manipulation. When romance feels like bait in sport fishing, we swim away to avoid being reeled in as someone's trophy catch.

This kind of self-centered romance is both fleeting and defeating. It is the stuff upon which flings and one-night stands are made of, but not a lasting marriage. Forming a relationship around a passing, insincere attraction doesn't create a lasting loving bond. So, should romance be abandoned? Hold on.

You are here reading this and will soon discuss your perspective with your partner because you felt their love was sincere.

How do we trust the place of romance in marriage? Is it a valid attachment or a dangerous entrapment? I'm going to argue that romance is measured primarily by its motives. Healthy romance is about caring for the other person first and foremost. It is giving. Unhealthy romance is about me – first and foremost. It is taking. Remember, it is better to give than to receive.

Naturally, we long to be loved in return for our romantic gestures toward our mate. But your focus should be on knowing that healthy romance is an unadulterated gesture of loving the person for who they are and not what we get in return. Real love is based on a personal choice, not being forced. Authentic romance reflects this.

But what about for those people who are romantically challenged? Or what happens when you think you've lost that loving feeling? Romance can be a type of infatuation that is short-lived. Once the ideal catch is landed, the pursuit is often over. No more bait is needed. Romantic actions can often fade and soon the romance dies.

Relational research shows that the rush of emotional adrenaline – the romantic "in love" feeling – lasts an average of between six and twenty-four months into the marriage (Marriage.com, 2022). What then? What can we do to help it grow beyond the early years of marriage? Can we learn to do romance right and keep it going long into your marital future? I think so. We challenge you to take steps to make romance a life-long experience as you begin your new marriage.

First, let's make sure we are on the same page. To me, romance is the expression of tender emotions and thoughtful gestures of devotion. It is the intentional and intense adventure that confirms attraction and creates attachment. To master this art for those who may be romantically challenged, it would be wise to focus on the following principles.

Romance is ESSENTIAL. It keeps your love alive. Special treatment of your life partner is what drew you together. Don't make assumptions. The deterioration of a relationship begins when you start taking your partner for granted. Ongoing affirmation of love creates a security and a closeness that make for a good marriage. Keep pampering, talking, having fun together and engaging as friends and lovers.

Romance is EFFORT. Make no mistake. Romance is work but it has its rewards. It involves making intentional and consistent attempts to express your devotion. To romance well, you go out of your way to show kindness and even practical help. Clean the kitchen. Wash his car. Write a note. Buy flowers. You simply must go out of your way to express love.

Romance is EXCLUSIVE. The heart of romance in marriage is the unique focus on one person above all others. If you are showing affection to many, you are not being romantic; you are a flirt and a cavalier. Real love needs to be single-minded. There are no rivals. The ring on the finger says so. Love is faithful.

Romance is EXTRAVAGANT. Lavash the one you love in whatever ways you can. Make the trivial significant. Make the little details matter. Denying yourself is normal. Saving extra to lavish a big surprise is common. Healthy romance is impractical, over the top and yet perfect because you know your spouse so well. You write a song or plan an evening. You surprise them with a getaway overnight. You know exactly what they love and you deliver. You lavish your love even if it seems crazy to others.

Romance is ENTICING. It keeps your spouse coming back to you. Romance is attractive. To feel wanted, appreciated and exclusive is what we all crave. It is as predictable as a moth to a porch light. The draw of attention and affection will keep your marriage strong to last long. You'll never regret any efforts you make towards romancing your partner.

Romance is ENDANGERED. You may say, "I'm not romantic." I challenge you that lack of romantic intention is both careless and dangerous neglect. Love always takes an effort. Turn this trend of a romanceless relationship around by thinking of the things that your spouse enjoys. Now demonstrate them in detail. Putting in the time and making an effort shows your partner they matter. Don't let your marital love fade though some others may.

You'll never regret continuing to put your marriage first by keeping the romance alive.

DISCUSSION STARTERS:

1. What do you feel are the top three romantic ways your spouse has shown that they really know and love you?

   -
   -
   -

2. What are three gestures or activities that you know really scream to your mate that you love them?

   -
   -
   -

3. What aspects of romance do you feel you need more of from your mate? List two and share them.

   -
   -

Chapter 20
Spring Cleaning of the Soul:
How Baggage Clutters Your Relational Freedom
Dr. Dave Currie

Early April is usually the time of year for Spring-cleaning. It is called so because of the urge most have for a new beginning. We really want to deal with the clutter and tackle the needed cleanup in our homes after a long winter. But what about cleaning up the clutter in our lives? Do you need some Spring-cleaning of the soul? Maybe. Read further...do you have clutter?

A stranger raped her on a summer job at a national park entrance gate. He was nine when he discovered his nineteen-year-old brother hanging dead in his bedroom after more drug-related drama. She raised herself and her brothers as her single mother was either working long hours or partying late. His parents told him he was useless and wished he was never born. Her older brother molested her. Alcoholic parents. Fighting parents. Absent parents. Critical parents. Drunk parents. Mentally ill parents. Divorced parents. Sick parents. Cheating parents. These experiences leave an imprint on the soul – especially if a pre-teen. These hard events or long-standing unhealthy situations create deep hurts often called emotional baggage. Each situation creates a story – and your story creates you.

There's more.

Beyond your family of origin trauma, what about the choices you make as you mature – your teen years and beyond? These decisions are equally complicating to your soul baggage and personal freedom. For instance, he became hooked on porn at fourteen and battles with it today. After huge fights with parents, she ran away with a boy at seventeen, staying at a flophouse a few nights. He cheated at school to make it through. She was sexually active at age fifteen and has been ever since. He messed with a lot of drugs. She battles with depression and attempted suicide twice. He can't keep a job. She's in big debt. He's a PlayStation addict. She's binging and purging. He gambles his paycheck away. Drinking problems. Using people. And on it goes. Each choice shapes a person's story – and your story decisions further complicate you.

HOW EMOTIONAL BAGGAGE AFFECTS ME?

Though your story may not qualify for a "Jerry Springer" TV show, your baggage definitely affects you. And face it – we all have some baggage, and it impacts us more than we care to admit. Keep in mind this life truth. "We are the sum total of those who have loved us or refused to love us". During those formative years, that sense of being loved is central to our success in future relationships. Without it, we'll have hurtful baggage and often unhealthy behaviors.

I believe that the number one problem in most marriages that struggle today is **the unresolved baggage brought into the relationship that tangles the couple's freedom** to love honestly, freely and selflessly.

Because our experiences and decisions are so interwoven into who we are and how we operate, we often don't see how much they have shaped our make-up. This "junk in our trunk" actually impacts how we view ourselves and the resulting steps we take interacting with others. Make no mistake – **dysfunction breeds dysfunction.** Unhealthy people can't approximate healthy relationships. Too much of the past is in the way. And the worst kind of baggage is that which is unperceived, unaddressed or denied. To become more aware of what issues you may be blind to, you will be challenged to fill out the **Baggage Check** at the end of this chapter.

WHAT IS BAGGAGE?

People often have only a vague notion of what this emotional clutter is. We'd be wise to agree on what we are talking about. Here's my working definition.

> *Baggage is the unresolved negative impact shaping who we are and how we interact caused by difficult events, tragic experiences or demanding people often from our family of origin and during our formative years. Baggage can also include the poor choices we make as teens and adults prior to our marriages that inhibit healthy relationships in our future.*

WHY DO WE AVOID SPRING-CLEANING OF THE SOUL?

Are you open to exploring what your baggage might be? Or maybe you think that you don't have any. But when you tell your story, do you tell all of it or do you hold back? What are you choosing to leave out? Most think, "Are you kidding? Won't bringing up your past – sharing things you're embarrassed about or deeply regret – only sabotage a relationship?"

Unhealthy fears do drive most of us to keep silent about our negative history. That's why, when it comes to baggage, denial is most common – people simply bury their past. They hide it from others and try to block it from their consciousness. Many downplay their experiences and say they were no big deal. Some attempt to discount the impact claiming the events have had no effect on them. One can seriously doubt the value of talking about baggage since it occurred so long ago and it won't change what happened. Sometimes hiding the truth either out of pain or shame seems best. After all, no one needs to know. And some of our past feels too difficult or painful to bring up.

Problem. Refusing to face negative past experiences is only half the concern. The other complication is the common inability to connect past baggage to present behavior. Thus, the term "blind spots". We don't see our issues or are just so used to acting in a certain way. It's been this way so long. If you downplay or deny baggage, you really have to deny any possible ongoing effect on your life – your reactions and emotions.

To become more aware of the effect your baggage may still be having on your life today, you have the opportunity to fill out the **Behavior Check** at the end of this chapter.

HOW TO BEGIN SPRING-CLEANING?

1. **BRAVELY FACE YOUR CLUTTER – THE SOONER THE BETTER.** Don't doubt whether or not your unresolved baggage affects how you live today. It does. And admission is the beginning of healing. Regardless of the source of your baggage, don't wait any longer to start dealing with it. Commit to finding the freedom to love others freely and fully.

   Trust what Jesus said: "Then you will know the truth and the truth will set you free. If the Son sets you free, you are free indeed." John 8:32,36

2. **SURRENDER YOUR LIFE TO GOD TO HEAD UP YOUR CLEAN UP.**
   Jesus makes all the difference in the world. There's hope. Ask Him to help you gain freedom from the trauma and hurts of your past. If you are feeling overwhelmed, remember He knows what you are carrying. Trust Him for strength and perspective.

   "Then Jesus said, 'Come to me, all of you who are weary and carry heavy burdens, and I will give you rest. Take my yoke upon you. Let me teach you, because I am humble and gentle at heart, and you will find rest for your souls.'" Matt. 11:28, 29

   "Give all your worries and cares to God, for he cares about you." 1 Peter 5:7

3. **STOP MAKING EXCUSES FOR THE MESS.** Take an honest look at the negative experiences that may have shaped you. Fill out the Baggage Check honestly. Remember, it's your life and your future. Even where others have caused real hurt to you; it does you no good to blame them any longer. Take responsibility for your attitudes and behavior from this point on. Make it your goal to become who God wants you to be.

   What happened may not be your fault – but it is still your responsibility to address it.

   "No, dear brothers, I am still not all I should be, but I am bringing all my energies to bear on this one thing: Forgetting the past [by dealing with the past] and looking forward to what lies ahead, [14] I strain to reach the end of the race and receive the prize for which God is calling us up to heaven because of what Christ Jesus did for us." Philippians 3:13-14

4. **START CLEANING UP YOUR LIFE.** Make amends where needed. Apologize if you have wronged someone. Do your part to rebuild relationships that are broken. Extend forgiveness whether asked to or not. Do what you can to address your past remembering that restoring relationships takes two willing parties. Do what depends on you.

   "If it is possible, as far as it depends on you, live at peace with everyone." Romans 12:18

5. **FIGHT FOR FULL FREEDOM FROM THE CLUTTER.** Be committed to do whatever it takes to get real peace with God and restoration with others on the issues you have to face. Fill out the Behavior Check. Work at making all the changes needed. Ask people you trust to help you connect the dots between your past baggage and your current actions and

attitudes. Get their support. Let your partner and a friend fill out the Behavior Check on you. Listen to what they see.

"Make this your common practice: Confess your sins to each other and pray for each other so that you can live together whole and healed. The prayer of a person living right with God is something powerful to be reckoned with." James 5:16

6. **COMMIT TO PROFESSIONAL HELP AS NEEDED.** Rather than continuing to struggle with the ongoing impact of the baggage you are carrying, wisdom says get the help to address it once and for all. The hurt and trauma needs to be processed. Deeply ingrained unhealthy patterns need to be identified and adjusted. Find a trusted pastor or counselor who can assist you in securing your freedom. What a gift to your spouse and the future of your marriage.

"Where there is no [wise, intelligent] guidance, the people fall [and go off course like a ship without a helm], But in the abundance of [wise and godly] counselors there is victory." Proverbs 11:14 AMP

"Without good direction, people lose their way; the more wise counsel you follow, the better your chances." Proverbs 11:14 MSG

Bravely address your baggage. Don't let it hamper your marriage or inadvertently pass it on to your children. Trust the Lord every step of the way in your life recovery journey. Get started today on the Spring Cleaning of your Soul.

DISCUSSION STARTERS:

1. Make 2 copies of the Baggage Check and the Behavior Check to use with others before you fill them in yourself.

2. Now, fill out the Baggage Check and the Behavior Check. Bravely do it because you want your personal freedom and because it is only fair to disclose your story openly to the one you love. Caution: don't live in denial or be dishonest by skipping over issues you have experienced.

3. Agree on a time to share with each other's Baggage and Behavior Checks. Listen. Support. Work to understand. Don't get defensive.

4. Allow your spouse and a good friend to use a second copy of the Behavior Check to identify the behaviors that they see and feel in you. Agree on a time to hear what they are seeing in you. Work hard to listen and not be defensive. This will not be easy.

5. Honestly admit that there may be a number of issues it would be wise for you to work through with a counselor. Call to make the appointment – this week – the sooner the better.

Personal Baggage Check

Dr. Dave Currie

Instructions: It is important to understand how harmful events and situations contribute to the shaping of your worldview, your relationships and your view of yourself. Acknowledging these challenges allows you to better face their effects on your life. Baggage can originate from hurtful experiences with parents, extended family, spouses, significant others, authority figures, friends and even strangers. Some baggage results from our own poor choices and negative patterns of behavior. **Underline** the issues that you have clearly experienced and **star*** any issues that you can partly identify with. Share the stories of your personal baggage with each other.

POSSIBLE SOURCES OF BAGGAGE

1. Abandoned/neglected as a child
2. Adopted
3. Alcoholic parent(s)
4. Anxiety/panic attacks
5. Bad choices in friendships
6. Been bullied/picked on
7. Broken engagement(s)
8. Broken trust in others
9. Bullied others
10. Caused accidental death
11. Caused an abortion
12. Caused serious injury
13. Cheated on by spouse
14. Chronic tension/stress
15. Controlling parents
16. Controlling spouse or partner
17. Criminal behavior/charges
18. Cult or occult involvement
19. Death of child/spouse
20. Death of significant other
21. Depression periods
22. Difficult child custody battle
23. Disabilities – physical/learning
24. Drinking problems/alcoholism
25. Drug addiction
26. Drug-addicted parent(s)
27. Early Pornographic exposure
28. Early sexual encounters
29. Emotional affair(s)
30. Experienced spiritual abuse/harm
31. Ex-spouse stresses
32. Extramarital affair(s)
33. Faced tragic accident/incidents
34. Failing marriage
35. Family image pressures
36. Felt abandoned by church
37. Fighting with parents
38. Financial loss or pressures
39. Gambling addiction
40. Gaming addiction
41. Gave child up for adoption
42. Had a divorce
43. Had an abortion
44. Harsh religious upbringing
45. Harsh treatment/discipline
46. Hated by peers/siblings
47. High expectations by parent(s)
48. Infertility/miscarriage(s)
49. Job loss
50. Lack of parental support
51. Legalistic upbringing
52. Let down by God or my faith
53. Lied to/manipulated by parent(s)
54. Lived with fear of harm
55. Lied to by spouse
56. Manipulated or lied to others
57. Mental breakdowns or hospitalized
58. Neglect of life basics–food, clothing
59. Parent(s) had affairs
60. Parent(s) with psychiatric problems
61. Parents fighting
62. Parents' divorce
63. Health issues/problems
64. Pawn between divorcing parents
65. Personality disorder(s)
66. Physical abused by others
67. Physically abused others
68. Poorly modeled relationships
69. Pornographic addiction
70. Premarital pregnancy
71. Premarital sexual activity
72. Prescription drug dependency
73. Previous marriage(s)
74. Rage or threats by parents
75. Raised in foster home(s)
76. Raised with step-siblings
77. Ran away from home
78. Raped by stranger
79. Raped by a date
80. Raped someone
81. Rejection by parents
82. Repeated failures
83. Repeated putdowns at home
84. School failure(s)/quit
85. Serious car accident/at fault
86. Serious family health issues
87. Sexually abused a child
88. Sexually abused by others
89. Sexual preoccupation/addiction
90. Sexually pressured a peer
91. Sibling rivalry/comparison
92. Spousal abuse
93. Step-parent rejection
94. Step-parenting stress
95. Suicidal attempts
96. Unhealthy dating patterns
97. Unrealistic expectations by parents
98. Unresolved conflict with family
99. Verbally abused/put down
100. Other issue:_____

_____

_____

Personal Behavior Check

Dr. Dave Currie

Instructions: What is the weight of your baggage? You need to unpack these. The following words describe negative behaviors and dispositions that are often the unhealthy reactions to events and situations from a person's history. Go through the list and bravely circle any of these attitudes or actions you admit could apply to you in the last three years. Then, underline the ones that you have seen in your fiancé or new spouse. Be as honest as possible in working toward a personal freedom for you and a growing relationship together. Share your observations with each other.

THE WEIGHT OF YOUR BAGGAGE

1. Abusive to others
2. Alcohol dependency
3. Angry outbursts
4. Bitter/resentful
5. Blaming others
6. Can't trust authorities
7. Can't/won't apologize
8. Confrontational
9. Critical
10. Critical self-talk
11. Cutting or self-abuse
12. Dangerous actions
13. Deceitful/lying
14. Deeply private, hiding feelings
15. Defensiveness
16. Denial of issues
17. Depression
18. Deserving punishment
19. Deviant sexual attractions
20. Distance from family relationships
21. Domineering/controlling
22. Doubting of God
23. Drug addiction
24. Eating disorder(s)
25. Emotional breakdown
26. Exploitation of others
27. Extreme weight issues
28. Fatalistic perspective
29. Fear of abandonment
30. Fear of commitment
31. Fear of disclosure
32. Fear of failure
33. Fear of intimacy-physical or emotional
34. Feeling unworthy of love

35. Freely condemning
36. Having to win
37. High anxiety
38. Hoarding/stealing
39. Homosexual confusion
40. Hopelessness
41. Inability to cope
42. Inability to have sex
43. Insecurity
44. Intolerance
45. Irrational fears
46. Lack of initiative
47. Live a façade/hidden
48. Low self-worth
49. Low sexual desire
50. Manipulative
51. Many health issues
52. Name-calling
53. Need independence
54. Need control
55. Need to perform
56. Panic attacks
57. Perfectionism
58. Porn addiction
59. Prescription drug abuse
60. Proud/condescending
61. Refusal to talk about past
62. Self-denial
63. Selfish/self-centered
64. Sense of failure
65. Sense of unworthiness
66. Sexual dysfunction
67. Sleeplessness
68. Suicidal thoughts

69. Timid/fearful
70. Unable to accept love
71. Unable to focus
72. Unwilling to forgive
73. Untrusting of others
74. Unwilling to risk
75. Withdrawal from others
76. Other _____
77. Other _____

Chapter 21
Conflict Resolution:
Steps to a Fair Fight
Jody Wandzura

When moving into our first home, Chris and I had to decide what should go where. We were standing in the kitchen surrounded by boxes. I found the one that contained cutlery and opened the top drawer where I thought our utensils should reside. I was in "go-mode" and expecting to get all the boxes unpacked in one day until I faced my first hurdle: "The cutlery should not go in that drawer; it should go in this drawer." At first, I thought he was kidding, but I realized he was serious. And the disagreement began.

Keeping calm and smiling sweetly, I simply stated in a factual voice that I had lived independently for five years already, and therefore, my understanding of kitchens was better than his. I started to put the spoons away. Things slightly escalated. Chris matter-of-factly retorted that he had been living in this house for the two months before the wedding and, therefore, had a better idea of what should go where. He added that I was wrong and why he was *right*. Wait. What? How is that possible? I am never wrong. Not only was he claiming to have the better idea, but he dared to suggest that I was *wrong*. He was obviously mistaken, so I repeated myself in a much firmer and faster voice, explaining again why my idea was better and why I should have the final say in this situation. He responded with the rhetorical question, "Does it always have to be your way?" Whoa. Now, it was personal. I was fuming and feeling hurt.

The simple conflict about which drawer should hold the cutlery turned into a downward spiral of fury. It started with finding the most practical location. It morphed into needing to win, was fueled by selfishness and ended with me retreating to the bedroom in anger and isolation. Have you been there before? We sure have.

About six years later, I heard a fantastic quote from Dr. Kenford Nedd, an author and speaker. He claimed, "Do you want to be right, or do you want to be loved?" I laughed at the cute quote, but it wasn't until later that it sunk in and made me think. The saying meant I can't push to win and still expect to be loved. Those two concepts do not go together. With each year of marriage, I was winning more of the arguments (in my mind, at least) and slowly losing my connection with my husband.

At this same time, Chris and I were working on a final relationship education project for our Master's degrees in Leadership. Ironically, while researching many communication and conflict resolution books, we miscommunicated and had more arguments than ever! The truth was that we had yet to establish healthy conflict-resolution patterns in our marriage. This project slapped us in the face and forced us to start applying what we were learning.

After over twenty years of creating problems, learning from our mistakes, and intentionally applying our new skills, we have significantly improved working through our differences. We still have arguments, but disagreements about trivial topics like cutlery are resolved quickly and efficiently. We have also improved in overcoming more complicated problems, but I am the first to admit we are far from perfect. We have condensed our conflict resolution strategy into these four steps to increase effectiveness.

#1. Search Yourself

Before addressing any issue in our relationship – even as insignificant as cutlery – we must humbly search our hearts for pride or sinful motives. This concept comes from Psalms, where David writes to God, saying, *"You have searched me, Lord, and you know me. You know when I sit and when I rise; you perceive my thoughts from afar. You discern my going out and my lying down; you are familiar with all my ways. Before a word is on my tongue, you, Lord, know it completely. Search me, God, and know my heart; test me and know my anxious thoughts. See if there is any offensive way in me, and lead me in the way everlasting."* (Psalm 139:1-4, 23-24) We need to ask God to help us search our hearts daily.

We also need to follow God's plan for relationships. The Bible asks us to serve one another, put the other person's needs ahead of our own, admit we are wrong, turn from our selfishness and address our anger before the sun goes down. That list creates high expectations for how we treat each other! To resolve conflict, we must ask God for self-control, selflessness and humility to follow His plan.

Unfortunately, this step is too often skipped or ignored. When we jump to Step #2, we show up with our boxing gloves on, opting out of the love approach and coming to win. (This is true for me, anyway.) Instead, if we take some time to reflect on our motives and pray about our thoughts, words, and actions, then God will show us where we need to change. Let's choose love so our relationship has a fighting chance!

#2. Set the Scene: Why, When, and Where

Before you meet with the other person, setting the scene when attempting conflict resolution is essential. Many of these basics are mentioned in communication chapters, which is why this chapter comes after those. Before solving a conflict, figure out the why, when and where to discuss.

> WHY
> "Why" is the most critical question of the three and the best opening statement to humbly set the scene. Take time to think about what you value. Determine if the relationship is meaningful enough to sort things out – even if it requires hard work and extra time. In my relationship with my husband, we have decided that there is never an issue we can't work through. It could sound like this: *"Our relationship is significant to me, and I want to do whatever it takes to resolve this issue."*
>
> Next, consider what is wrong between you and how this makes you feel. How do you wish the relationship would be? It could sound like this: *"I don't like how things feel between us, and I am sorry for my part in this."*

WHEN

Ask the other person, *"When would be a good time to talk this through?"* You must give yourself enough time to think things through, search your heart and be at your best for the discussion. Sometimes, time and space are all you need to resolve the problem.

WHERE

Also, agree on the location by asking, *"Where would be the best place to meet?"* Face-to-face meetings always seem more efficient and effective. There are times when distance or schedules make it impossible to meet, so flexibility in format may be essential. On occasion, you might need to settle for a phone call or Zoom meeting.

#3. Share Your Sides: Express, Listen and Swap

Whenever you communicate, you need to remember the fundamental concepts of expressing and listening that you read in the earlier chapters. Here is the overview:

EXPRESS

Take time to formalize what you will say thoughtfully. Choose kind words and a warm, respectful tone. One person will take their turn fully sharing their side before the other speaks. They can start by saying, *"I have thought a lot about our disagreement last night and would like to share things from my perspective. When I finish, I would like to hear yours."*

If the issue is severe or causing great hurt, start your sharing time by praying together. You could ask the other person, *"Before I begin, would it be ok if I ask God for His help?"* Commit your relationship to God by saying, *"God, we give you our relationship. We value it so much and want it to be protected and strengthened. Please help us be unselfish and work through this problem to find a wise and peaceful solution. Amen."*

If the issue is complicated or you feel nervous about sharing your thoughts, write these items out ahead of time and read them. It could sound like this: *"Sometimes I fumble my words, so I have taken the time to write them out and will read them to you."*

LISTEN

Maintain eye contact, be distraction-free and nod when you understand. Remain focused and listen to the end of the message. The only verbal interjections allowed are clarifying questions, reflecting comments or paraphrasing statements.

SWAP

The first speaker can say, *"I have fully shared my perspective. Thank you for listening."* Then, the two people trade roles, and the second person may express their side with the first person listening intently.

#4. Select Your Solution: ME-Solution or WE-Solution

There are two resolutions to any dispute: the ME-Solution and the WE-Solution. Once you feel heard and understood, both people must consider, *"What can I do to solve this problem?"* The ME-Solution is when an individual decides to personally take responsibility for making changes and accommodations to fix the problem.

The WE-Solution is when both give a little. Each person slightly compromises their desires to serve the other and improve the relationship. Each person can reply, "I would be willing to..." or ask, "Would you be willing to...?" When each of you comes willing to be the ME-Solution, you will quickly turn it into a WE-Solution. You are never allowed to demand a YOU-Solution.

At the end of the discussion, it is okay to take a day or so to think about things further before finalizing the outcome. Be sure to agree on the delay to finish the discussion. Be sure to end by praying and thanking God for his help.

The more you search your heart, employ excellent communication skills, and practice these steps in resolving conflict, the quicker and more efficiently you can manage every disagreement.

DISCUSSION STARTERS:

1. Take time to search your heart on how you've been discussing the significant problems. Are you a humble person who tries to put your spouse's needs ahead of your own?" Write down how you perceive yourself.

2. Who wins most of your arguments? If one person claims this title, please discuss why. Do you have equal time to share? Do each of you feel heard? Discuss this...

3. Consider the phrase, "A couple who prays together stays together." How often do you pray about your conflicts? Why or why not? Do you pray individually or as a couple?

4. As an extension of this chapter on Conflict Resolution, take time to work through the following "Rules of Engagement." Work separately and then come together as instructed.

Rules of Engagement:

Dr. Dave Currie

Determine your Rules of Engagement by circling six principles that would be the greatest help to resolve issues in your marriage. Then star the three that are non-negotiable of those six. Share and discuss your selections and agree on a combined list of the top eight. Write them out and post them in a place where you both can see them regularly.

Choose Your Rules of Engagement

1. Bravely admit there are issues to discuss – don't avoid them or run away.
2. Don't downplay or dismiss what your spouse sees as an important issue.
3. Focus on the shared goal of a great marriage and commit to grow closer.
4. Pray together for God's guidance on the problems we are facing.
5. Agree on a specific time/place to talk through issues – don't jump into it.
6. Get alone to engage on problems – not in front of others, especially kids.
7. Share your commitment to work through the issue fairly and respectfully.
8. Remind each other out loud, "You are not my enemy."
9. Admit the unresolved anger and hurts from past fight failures. Clear the air.
10. Sit down to solve issues. Avoid standing or pacing. Give undivided attention.

11. Stay on one topic at a time until resolution. Don't introduce a second issue.
12. Observe equal voice: Give uninterrupted time to share feelings and frustrations.
13. Share your perspective without assuming you are right. Pack your pride.
14. Really listen and work to understand the other's perspective. Show empathy.
15. Use "I" statements when explaining yourself – Don't assign blame.
16. Speak the truth lovingly, honestly and without manipulation.
17. Show mutual respect by talking calmly and kindly – don't raise your voice.
18. Express your strong opinions or negative emotions responsibly. Don't unload!
19. Don't force instant solutions by pushing for a decision to get your own way.
20. Discuss the problem – don't attack the person. Don't cause hurt.

21. List possible solutions/options and decide together on a course of action.
22. Work to compromise and accommodate when possible to get a win-win.
23. Don't walk out unless you need a "time out". Explain it before you step away.
24. If frustrations/tensions are causing hurt, agree on a time to talk later.
25. Stop long before any verbal or physical abuse can get started.
26. Allow no harsh words, sarcastic remarks, swearing, threats or ultimatums.
27. Humble yourself to accept responsibility and apologize. Ask for forgiveness.
28. Maintain a willingness to forgive fully and freely – let the offense go.
29. Hold on tight to each other – the marriage is more important than the issue.
30. Seek outside help to resolve conflicts before things blow up.

Record your selections and then agree on your combined top 8 rules:

His Numbers: ___ ___ ___ ___ ___ ___

Her Numbers: ___ ___ ___ ___ ___ ___

Combined: ___ ___ ___ ___ ___ ___ ___ ___

CONFLICT RESOLUTION SUCCESS

What does a **victory** in overcoming friction look and feel like for you? From the following measurements of victory, choose two and then discuss why they are important to you. Then agree on the two that are most important to keep as a couple to measure success in your conflict resolution.

1. Feeling Heard and Understood
2. Unity on the Issue
3. A Good Solution/Direction
4. Both Feel the Decision is Good
5. Issue Got Resolved Finally
6. Genuine apology given.
7. Forgiveness extended
8. Decision Honors God
9. Peace Between Us
10. Sense of Well-Being
11. A Win-Win Solution
12. Free to Love and Be Friends
13. Didn't Compromise my Values
Other: _____

Her 2:   ____ ____

His 2:   ____ ____

Our 2:   ____ ____

REMEMBER: Your goal is to become a UNITED FRONT against the inevitable problems that will arise in your marriage and to never again target your spouse as the enemy.

Chapter 22
Merging Grace:
The Art of Two Becoming One
Dr. Dave Currie

"For this reason, a man will leave his father and mother and be united to his wife, and __the two will become one__ flesh." Mark 10:8

Two becoming one. Great concept but easier said than done. For this relational connection to best happen after a wedding, merging grace must surface early and sustain long as the non-negotiable principle behind two people whose goal is being joined as one.

Merging grace. It's a struggle for me; ask my wife.

By nature, I am independent, selfish and demanding. Like now, during a recent, nearby bridge construction project, with my competitive nature, I am more likely to speed up in traffic and cut in (even cut you off) than to slow down and let you go first. To 'merge' seems to take something I don't automatically have.

Yet, I have seen what "merging grace" in a marriage looks like, and it looks amazing.

Merging grace is seen clearly in the now-dated show, "Dancing with the Stars." But you know how it goes. The winning pair of professional and celebrity is a magnificent combination of fluid motion and dynamic unity. The blending of talent and strength is seamless in its choreography and displays oneness in mind and movement. The dancers seem to know what the other is thinking, anticipate their next move and are always complementing each other – never competing. They engage, encourage and esteem their partners to bring the best out of each other. They don't win alone. When their dance is done right, they are conscious of not stepping on the other's toes and usually end in an embrace. Brilliant!

That is a great picture of a fabulous marriage with *merging grace*. But what do you do if you resemble the grace of King Kong?

I am defining "merging grace" (my own words) as the choice to compassionately and selflessly blend your life with that of your mate's. On one hand, it is making an effort to offer yourself and your thoughts freely and frequently so you have an equal voice. On the other, you quiet your confidence to include your spouse by really listening with the goal of real collaboration. The grace to merge may be best expressed when I love when they don't deserve it, when I keep trying to understand and when I forgive freely. In becoming one magnificent, integrated dance, we reflect God's plan. By doing so, we end up enjoying the marriage more too.

It is moving from "me" to "we". Trite but true. Research maintains on average it takes about 10 years of marriage for a person to get over himself (FamilyLife Marriage, 2001). I wish it was that short. I find that the deeper the selfishness, the grander the arrogance and the stronger the independence, the longer the journey takes toward really merging.

I have haunting memories of my graceless attempts at merging. Selfish, blaming, arguing and not listening well. I claim full rights to "jerkhood" for the first five years of our marriage (my wife maintains at least six). The problem even lingered beyond our twenty-fifth wedding anniversary as I distinctly remember asking God for one whole year to *'please make me into a man who is gracious'*. It was actually written in the front of my Day-Timer (yes, back in the day when paper ruled).

As a Type A personality, we aren't the only ones who struggle to merge. To withhold yourself and your perspective from your spouse out of insecurity or fear equally thwarts the connection. It's too easy to hesitate and be compliant and then to blame your partner if things don't go well. Don't wait for all the stars to align before you share yourself – do so, and the sooner the better.

What if you are impatient, critical and driven to excellence? In this case, you have more than a little arrogance about your perspective. You over-value your views and question your spouse's input. Merging is equally hard if you are insecure and indecisive and don't think you have something to offer. You tend to devalue yourself and the input you can give.

If you are like me, you have heard your share of people saying that marriage reveals how selfish you really are. Merging is more than tough stuff when you add coming from different backgrounds, histories, likes and dislikes, hobbies, pastimes and beliefs. We haven't even touched on diverse personalities.

Someone once mused, "Yeah, right. Two become one alright – but which one?"

How can two dance as one and move their relationship toward being seamless and inclusive? Below are the practical steps that will help get you there. But first, catch God's heart on the matter in the following verses. And oh my, what a difference these principles would make if truly applied!

> "Here is a simple, rule-of-thumb guide for behavior: Ask yourself what you want people to do for you, then grab the initiative and do it for *them*." Matthew 7:12 (MSG)

> "If you've gotten anything at all out of following Christ, if his love has made any difference in your life, if being in a community of the Spirit means anything to you, if you have a heart, if you *care*— then do me a favor: Agree with each other, love each other, be deep-spirited friends. Don't push your way to the front; don't sweet-talk your way to the top. Put yourself aside, and help others get ahead. Don't be obsessed with getting your own advantage. Forget yourselves long enough to lend a helping hand." Phil. 2:1-4 (MSG)

> "Let your conversation be gracious and attractive so that you will have the right response for everyone." Col. 4:6 (NIV)

STEPS TOWARD MERGING GRACIOUSLY IN MARRIAGE:

1. **LET GOD BE THE CATALYST:** You need Him dearly to help you merge well in your marriage. Only He can reveal and root out the innate selfishness or paralyzing fears we often possess. Braid God in daily.

2. **FIGHT FOR EACH OTHER:** Accept that moving from ME to WE is far harder than we think. Remain committed to work through every stress and never give up on the "US". A good marriage is worth the work.

3. **GIVE UP YOUR INDEPENDENCE:** Lay down your solo agenda to blend your lives into one. Don't try to win arguments – win at understanding. Integrate, don't annihilate. Find a win-win solution whenever possible!

4. **VALIDATE EACH OTHER'S PERSPECTIVES:** Respect and value the unique opinion your spouse will bring. Believe that God brought you a life partner as a valued compliment to who you are and what you know. Listen well to them.

5. **ENGAGE YOUR VIEWPOINT:** Believe that God doesn't make junk and that your contribution matters. Stronger and better marriages are when both perspectives are integrated in marital decisions.

6. **OWN YOUR STUFF:** Past personal and relational baggage surfaces in marriage as in no other relational context. Deal with both your hurts and your personality quirks. The sooner you share with your spouse about issues that inhibit you, the better.

7. **FORGIVE TO A FAULT:** Be patient with the changes needed. Make allowance for each other's imperfections. Always try to show love and kindness. Give your spouse the benefit of the doubt. Forgive freely and often.

Believe that God brought you together and that His plan is not just for you to receive His saving grace for life but His merging grace for a great marriage.

DISCUSSION STARTERS:

1. What ways have you seen evidence of your independence and selfishness in your marriage? Share a few of these.

    •

    •

2. What could you do to better listen to and integrate your partner's perspective in life decisions and directions?

    •

    •

3. Write out 2 things do you need from your spouse to feel more heard and understood?

    •

    •

4. Agree to take this merger to the Lord in prayer together asking Him to help you put your spouse's interests ahead of your own. Take time to do this now – as in right now at this present moment.

Chapter 23
God's Design for Intimacy:
The Purpose of Sex in Marriage
Dr. Dave Currie

It is important as you embark on marriage that you seek to develop a healthy and comprehensive perspective on the purposes of human sexuality and what God intended it to bring within the confines of committed marital love. The widespread view within society is so limited, selfish and frankly, skewed on its grasp of sex. It is paramount that you grow beyond such a negative, reductionistic view of sexuality. It should move toward one that embraces all that is possible for a vigorous and vibrant intimacy in a solid marriage.

Sex was God's idea. *He created sex, and He wants your future sexual intimacy in marriage to be AWESOME!* Remember: He created men and women as sexual creatures in the first place, and regarding His pinnacle of creation (humankind), He declared it was all *very good* – including the sexual capacity! Problem. Everything God creates as good, including sexuality, the enemy – Satan – tries to pervert, pollute or destroy. He tries to strip it of its meaning, its sanctity and its exclusiveness. Open your mind and heart to learn all that God envisioned marital sex to be (once you have cleared out the negative and selfish cultural view). Grow with me.

The Purposes of Sex in Marriage:

1. **To Proclaim Love** – The greater the love, the greater the freedom to share in the joy of holistic sexual expression through your trusted and caring connection. Great marital intimacy is comprehensive in its scope: it is relational, emotional, spiritual and yes, fully sexual. Sex is part of the full manifestation of "I Love You" not the sole representation or the highest sign of love. Focus on the goal toward "making love" with your spouse, not just "having sex" with them. Making love is designed to be relational where the partner is a person you love not an object you use. Love causes you to stay present, focusing on them during sexual experiences. Having sex is very self-absorbed and focuses on pushing to get personal needs met. That partner who is into him or herself, and is not present or in the moment, can often be in their own fantasy world letting their biological drive call the shots. It is often one-sided sex where the needs of both partners aren't being met. There can even be anger, blaming, pressuring, criticizing when it is merely about sex. This is not making love – not US. Rather, with love making, say by your actions and disposition: "I love you by being with you in this moment – we are sharing this mutually-fulfilling sensuous experience."

2. **To Promote Unity** – The Bible calls it *"ONENESS"*. There is such joy in this unique and exclusive expression of connection. It achieves a harmony in friendship like nothing else can. Imagine, as God intended, the husband will be united to his wife – the two becoming one flesh. And what God has brought together, let no one separate. Read it for yourself: *"But at*

the beginning of creation God 'made them male and female.' ⁷ 'For this reason a man will leave his father and mother and be united to his wife, ⁸ and the two will become one flesh.' So, they are no longer two, but one flesh. ⁹ Therefore what God has joined together, let no one separate" (Mark 10:6-9). This joining of bodies – the sexual act of intercourse – is this amazing symbolism of two becoming one! As God intended, it expresses full unity knowing 'I do this only with you'. There is literally, nothing between you – flesh on flesh – as your bodies are joined. When love making well, you are really close in every way and feel even closer afterwards. It is a very powerful and meaningful expression of the "US". It is deeply captivating to know, "I am unique to you and you are unique to me." Through joining of bodies, hearts and souls – We are ONE as God intended – unified. You are one flesh – unique – exclusive – just the two of you as ONE.

3. **To Produce Identity** – There is joy in being able to make love well. There is both delight and satisfaction in fulfilling your role as a sexual creature with your spouse. With the affirmation of being declared a good lover brings great personal satisfaction. It is true and should be that 'it is better to give than to receive.' Within marriage, being a good lover is certainly a significant part of life-verification of one's manhood or womanhood. There's no argument that it is true and right to say regarding your sexual experiences with your spouse: "You make me feel like a man or a woman". But that is only half of the equation. By giving love well and fully satisfying our spouse, it is equally true and right to say, "I make me feel like a man or a woman! – I loved you well." My identity as a sexual partner is established. Sexual manhood and sexual womanhood are now fully part of the picture. Loving well and being loved well impacts both our sexual identify and our self-worth. With healthy and mutual intimacy, we feel wanted. Valued. Needed. Fulfilled. Pursued. Competent. But learning to be a good lover is not automatic. Sexual intimacy in marriage was designed to be a shared growing experience where you learn together what pleases the other person. And in doing so, to feel good about yourself as a sexual partner. Sadly, this healthy perspective on marital love-making and what it does for our sense of well-being is frequently distorted by histories of sexual abuse, pornography exposure, and recreational sexual experiences. More often than not, personal love maps have been severely damaged before the couple comes into the marriage. Because of these types of narratives, a marriage partner can feel compared, evaluated and another "conquest" and not really loved. Work through the issues that may be preventing you from being able to love well.

4. **To Prevent Fornication** – A vibrant, meaningful and satisfying sex life in marriage is designed to keep the couple unified for life. FAITHFULNESS is a beautiful thing when couched between loyalty and trust. The passion of sexual desire is a powerful draw intended to keep you coming back for more. This joy of sexual loyalty is a give and take relationship. On one hand, a person experiences **the joy of staying faithful** to their spouse in part because their innate pure, God-given needs of love and sexuality are consistently, sufficiently and exclusively met in the relationship. On the other hand, that same spouse can experience **the joy of being faithful** by the way they are working to meet their spouse's sexual needs. Though not their responsibility alone, regular intimacy does assist the spouse in not looking elsewhere. 1 Corinthians 7:5,6: *"Do not deprive each other of sexual relations, unless you both agree to refrain from sexual intimacy for a limited time so you can give yourselves more completely to prayer. Afterward, you should come together again so that Satan won't be able to tempt you*

because of your lack of self-control." The point is clear. Don't deprive each other sexually so you might get tempted to go outside the marriage covenant to have sex with someone else. Satisfying and mutual sexual intimacy is designed to stop temptations to unfaithful involvement.

5. **To Please Passionate Urges** – Face it. There is great joy in sexual gratification. God has created men and women alike in that with the pleasure explosion associated with sexual orgasm, there is a powerful surge of adrenaline in the brain. This incredibly intoxicating chemical cocktail is as thoroughly addictive as the strongest drug addiction – cocaine included. With the release of all these endorphins and enkephalins, the dopamine and later, the oxytocin into the central amygdala – the pleasure center of the brain – there develops a 'craving for more' appetite – the reward-repeat cycle is set in motion. Since it feels good, the brain says, "Do that again." Remember, sex is God-created, and He set this adrenaline cycle in motion for a reason. The brain is wired chemically to seek to create further opportunities to re-experience the sexual surge of the orgasm. This is part of His plan to enjoy yourself in your sexual experiences for years to come. Yet, within humankind, unlike the animal kingdom, strong biological needs can still fall within the God-honoring moral structure of the brain – the prefrontal cortex – which causes us to behave and act wisely and faithfully. Animal-like urges don't have to rule. Human loyalty can win over lust. But within marriage, God wants you both to fully enjoy yourselves sexually. Aim at completely satisfying your mate.

6. **To Procreate/Children** – The joy of parenting cannot be over-estimated. Beyond Donalyn's and my marriage, our greatest blessing in life is the thrill of our ongoing engagement with our married children and our grandchildren. And that is God's plan for families. *"Children are a heritage from the LORD, offspring a reward from him" (Psalm 127:3).* They are an incredible gift from the Lord and the rewards of having them are clear. The sexual act under God's divine plan allows you to experience the miracle of a baby's development and birth. Just seeing the first breath is in itself breath-taking. Then, examining the mystery of that little body that is all functioning as designed is overwhelming. Then, there's the pride of holding your first child. You watch and observe every nuance of their growth: first smile, first giggle, first facial recognition of you, first audible sound, first words, walking, talking...hearing the words, "mama or dada" ... intoxicating. And you can add more children – blessing upon blessing. Not only do you get to experience the pride of it all as Mom and Dad, but if you parent well, they will be a gift that keeps on giving. The power of procreation is utterly astonishing.

God's plan for human sexuality is beautiful. His purposes are extensive and enriching. Broaden your heart and mind as you grow your sexual union with your spouse. Embrace the opportunity to fulfill all of His design for marriage.

DISCUSSION STARTERS:

1. Which one of the six purposes was a new concept to you? What did you like about it?

2. Which one of the six purposes seems the most important to you? Explain why.

3. Which one of the six purposes do you feel you will have the hardest time with? Explain why.

4. Discuss the six purposes one at a time to strengthen your reasons as a couple for developing a growing satisfying and mutual sex life in your marriage.

Chapter 24
Creating Healthy Boundaries to Protect Your Marriage

Jody Wandzura

When I visited my sister in rural Kentucky, I was intrigued by how different things were from where I lived in Canada's Fraser Valley of British Columbia. The scenery was unique, with the rolling hills and endless grassy plains. Some trees lined the roads, and scattered farmhouses dotted the land. The wind was more robust, churning up the dry, dusty ground.

What stood out the most from my surveillance was the lack of boundaries from one rural yard to the next. There were few fences, no land markers and no enclosures. How did the people know what belonged to them? How did they keep their pets at home and their children safe? Were they okay with going outside and having everyone watch them relax in their backyard? This fenceless society rather bothered me.

I thought more about why I value a boundary around my yard. I like knowing what is mine to enjoy and tend to – my grass to mow, flower beds to admire, edges to trim and yard to relax. A fence also makes me feel safe. Children can go into the back yard and play without any worries. If a stranger came in, they would run inside to find their parent. A fence is for our protection.

Another reason that I like a good, solid wall is for privacy and freedom. I love to be silly and I love to have fun! I want to play Spikeball and spin around between hits. When my children were tiny, I liked to sit in our kiddie pool to escape the heat of the summer. My kids love to drag a string for their Bengal cat to chase. My son and I play catch with a football or play catch with our baseball gloves. We play all of these things in the privacy of our backyard. There is no one to critique us. No one to judge us. Just the liberty to be our silly, active selves!

When I pondered these values, I realized there is a similar comparison between backyard fences and the boundaries of your most important relationship. Marriage is a precious commitment, so safeguards are paramount to preserve something valuable. Here are the boundaries you should create: time, relational and online.

TIME Boundaries

Let's face it! Life gets crazy, and our schedules are usually too full! Making time for each other needs to be non-negotiable. Being in the same room, like cleaning the kitchen together, does not count. Therefore, we must intentionally create both *daily and weekly* time boundaries. You need to reserve a certain amount of daily minutes to connect with a face-to-face conversation about life's impact – how your day was. It must be focused, alone time to slow down and reconnect.

You also need a blocked-off date night. Carving out a permanent slice of your week needs to be a priority in your life. Just you. Just me. Just being together. With kids under age six, every second week. This time boundary provides a sense that "this is our special time together, and nothing should impede it".

Over the years, our date night booking has morphed. Before we had kids, my husband and I always had our date nights on Saturday evenings, and nothing changed. When the kids were born, we booked a babysitter every other week on a Saturday night, which stayed consistent until they started getting involved in sports and other activities. Over the past eight to ten years, we have struggled to keep our date nights consistent as our lives revolve around our kids' schedules. We have had to learn to be flexible with which night we spend time together. Often, we have to move our date night to another night, and unfortunately, it sometimes gets pushed back to another week. Although we try hard to keep it etched in stone, we need to do a better job of planning to keep one date night per week.

RELATIONAL Boundaries

Relational boundaries guard against allowing anyone to take your spouse's relational, emotional or sexual place. This distraction can be a friend or co-worker – someone in your life for neutral reasons. At first, they were nothing more than an amiable colleague, helpful neighbor or caring friend. Still, compromises can quickly occur without proper safeguards.

In my early twenties, I witnessed a trespass that made me uncomfortable. At first, my boss would just chat with my co-worker in the hall, but then he would visit her office. I overheard him making jokes about his wife in a negative light. Soon, his visits became more frequent and throughout the day. He would be leaning against her desk, laughing out loud and staying after hours. She seemed to like the attention and didn't think anything was wrong with it as they were "just friends." I didn't like it and felt their spouses wouldn't like it either.

As life continued, my husband and I experienced many "out-of-bounds" situations that helped us develop the safeguards we now have. These examples can stimulate conversation and help you establish boundaries early in your marriage.

A new coach asked if he could talk to me about something private in my office. I said yes but felt uncomfortable when he closed the door behind himself, so before we began our conversation, I opened the blinds and stood right before the window. This created the "open door" safeguard.

Open Door Boundary: Being alone behind closed doors with someone of the opposite gender is not healthy for any relationship. My husband and I are both teachers, so we have created an "open door" policy when meeting students, co-workers, or parents of the opposite gender. I have a window in my office and always keep the blinds open. We also don't go into a house alone with a person of the other gender.

A lady at church shared a common interest with my husband. She offered her phone number to him so they could meet for coffee to discuss their shared interest further. Chris and I talked after church, and even though she may have good intentions, this created the "public outing" safeguard.

Public Outing Boundary: Spending time with someone else's spouse creates an eyebrow-raising appearance. We have agreed that we never go for dinner or coffee alone with someone of the opposite gender. Going as couples or in groups is better.

I had a neighbor pop over while I was mowing the lawn and tell me he wished he had a wife who would work hard like me and be more helpful in the yard and around the house. I thanked him for his compliment, but then I told him I didn't like how he put her down and that we should be thankful for our spouses. He never made another comment like that. This led to the "dirty laundry" safeguard.

Dirty Laundry Boundary: Sharing negative traits or stories about your spouse harms marriage. We have agreed that we will not complain about our partner's problems or faults with others as our perspective is often tainted, which makes the other person look like the bad guy! We also don't entertain listening to someone discuss their spouse's shortcomings.

A server in a restaurant walked by, and the man sitting at the table across from us completely turned his head to check out the back view of her extremely tight skirt. The lady sitting at the table with him pretended not to notice or care, but it made me thankful for Chris because he has never gawked at other women and has "eyes only for me."

Eyes for You Boundary: Sexually alluring images stay in your mind and can corrupt a desire for purity. My husband and I both try to look away from physically luring people. Doing this is especially meaningful to me when we go to a restaurant and the server is scantily clad. Chris does a great job of ordering quickly and never taking a second look.

Another neighbor stopped to talk while he was walking by with his kids. He shared that he and his wife were struggling and might get divorced. I told him I was sorry he was facing that, but I was not the one to share this with. I offered to get Chris, but he politely declined and left. This began a discussion between my husband and me on "depth of conversation."

Depth of Conversation Boundary: Like the layers of an onion, we all have levels of disclosure that we can peel back, but you should only reveal the intimate details with your spouse. When we work, coach, or spend time with someone of the opposite gender, my husband and I never discuss our personal lives or ask them about theirs. Instead, we keep it light, professional and polite; we only converse about the information needed for that assignment.

Relational boundaries become especially important if your marriage is in conflict or your spouse does not give you the desired attention. Suddenly, that person at work who is warm and caring may seem like a breath of fresh air. You appreciate their attention and welcome their presence. You try to be around them as often as possible. You may share your problems with them. They seem like a better option than your spouse.

Unfortunately, if your marriage is unhealthy and you don't have boundaries, that innocent friend may be allowed to replace your spouse. **Neediness + Carelessness = Unfaithfulness.** These signs need to be a red flag of warning to you to seek outside professional counsel to help your marriage regain a healthy status!

ONLINE Boundaries

Fishing is my least enjoyable activity as I don't prefer sitting still for long periods with little reward. The only thing I love about fishing is the lures. They are so fun to look at with all their bright colors, fake feathers, shiny dangles and sharp hooks. I can only imagine how alluring they are to a fish.

Social media has created increased communication accessibility and unprecedented bravery to say things you wouldn't dare say face-to-face. Like the fishing hooks, people cast out their seductive comments and pictures like sexual lures. They want attention or affirmation. What do you do when you receive a playful message from a fling from the past? Or how do you respond to a sexual compliment for something you posted? What about a provocative picture? They are harmless, aren't they?

Once, a co-worker messaged me to go to Starbucks to grab a coffee together since we were the "two most fun people on staff." My response was, "Who else is coming?" When he replied, "Just us," I asked if he didn't mind bringing me back a coffee instead. He was slightly annoyed with me, but he got the message. Social media allowed him extra bravery; he would have never invited me face-to-face.

When faced with out-of-line comments or invitations, you must tactfully choose to protect your prime relationship first by dismissing any unwanted offers. Reject and protect. If you shut the door immediately, you send this intruder a clear message that you are not interested in their extra attention and wish they would not continue.

Another safeguard is accessibility to harmful websites. The pornography industry has made sexually explicit content too convenient, and it is destroying many individuals and marriages. Do what is needed to block porn if it's a problem. There are also websites and apps for hook-ups, romantic encounters, or casual sex. It shouldn't have to be said, but any thoughts or actions towards unfaithfulness are a massive betrayal of trust in your relationship. Get off social media if others are a temptation. These need to be avoided (or confessed) at all costs.

One of the greatest gifts my parents ever gave me was a membership for a website blocking software. Although I have never been tempted by porn, I feel content knowing that no one in my house, including my kids or their friends, can view it either.

Like fences are to yards, boundaries are to marriages. What safeguards will *you* build to protect *your* marriage?

DISCUSSION STARTERS:

1. TIME boundaries: Do you have a chunk of time consistently carved out for your daily chat? What about your weekly dates? What can you do to ensure that these happen?

2. RELATIONAL boundaries: What are some basic guidelines in your relationship to protect you from unhealthy situations or people? Identify and create five relational boundaries.

   -
   -
   -
   -
   -

3. ON-LINE boundaries: What social media accounts do you each have? Do you have complete access to each other's accounts, including passwords? Discuss...

4. Have you ever gone on a pornographic website? What accountability or protection software do you have to avoid mistakenly or even intentionally visiting a questionable website?

Chapter 25
What Happens When a Couple Prays Together

Dr. Dave Currie

Praying together. It just sounds right. After all, shouldn't couples that are seeking God be reaching out regularly as one in prayer? This point touches a nerve in far too many of us. We are instantly uncomfortable. Many will skip this chapter. Pain avoidance. Why is there a disconnect with marital prayer?

WE'VE NEVER PRAYED TOGETHER

First off, it's a sad and all too common norm in many marriages. If you're like most Christian couples, you don't pray with your spouse either. Relational research shows that 92% of couples that call themselves Christians don't pray together (FamilyLife Survey, USA, 2001). There may be customary rituals at mealtime or a bedtime routine with the kids, but praying with your mate isn't happening. We seem to have a phobia-like aversion to this with a magnitude usually associated with things like spiders, snakes, or heights!

FACING YOUR PHOBIA

Why does praying together with your spouse evoke such great fear? Here are a few of the common reasons for the marital prayer phobia. First of all, many of us don't pray much on our own, so how could we ever make it work with our mate? Next, if you are at all insecure or private about your faith, you might avoid it because you aren't comfortable praying, feeling you don't know how, and fear judgment. On the other extreme, some are too proud and independent and feel like they don't need God. They think that prayer is for people who can't solve things on their own. I'd be careful – remember: pride comes before a fall (Proverbs 16:18). Further, doesn't praying together necessitate that you must be close to your mate and free of issues as a couple to commune at this deep level? Right. When will that ever happen? And finally, when reaching out to God is not a priority or preference to one or both of you, praying together can easily get squeezed out of our already busy lives. Face it, to pray together with your spouse will take a lot of commitment.

WHAT MARITAL PRAYER IS

What does a couple praying together look and feel like in real life? Here's the target I am proposing:

Couple prayer is a husband and wife, who, being honest with God and each other, join together regularly, despite their marital imperfections or personal brokenness, to humbly reach out to

116

Him for strength, direction and perspective. They go to God as one. They want His will for their lives and family.

Marital prayer is a step of faith you take together. Remember, you are both naked before God – he already and always, sees all and knows all – so worry less about your words. Get over yourselves. Admit you need the Lord in your lives (Proverbs 3:5,6). He knows you need Him far more than you do. Get your hearts right before Him. Your prayer together is an act of surrender to the God who is there, who cares and responds. Praying together is a good thing, especially in marriage.

BUT I SUCK AT PRAYING

But you say, "I am just not comfortable praying," or worse, "I suck at praying!" You weren't good at walking or riding a bike at first, either. The difference is you stayed at it. For some of you, you need to get used to hearing your own voice out loud when you pray. You may have to face the fear that someone beyond God is listening to you. You may need to overcome your worry about not getting the words right. Maybe you don't know what to pray. For some, you don't pray because you would rather avoid dealing with the issues between you and your spouse. May I suggest that you try – "just do it" (borrowing the Nike slogan). And look for specific help on this in the next chapter: "How to Start Praying Together."

THE BENEFITS OF PRAYING TOGETHER

Here are my top ten benefits of praying together and what it could do for your marriage:

1. **You'll hear and understand the heart of your spouse in prayer.** It will bring you a growing emotional connection. I met a man in his sixties who was thirty-seven years married if you add together both of his marriages. He had never prayed with either wife. Now, in wanting a sincerely Christian marriage, he took my challenge to start praying that night with his wife. The next morning, he was excited to report that they prayed together for the first time. He said, "I heard her heart. I know it will allow me to get closer to her. I am so excited." His experience is the truth.

2. **You'll face your stresses together at the deepest level.** Whether it's life or family problems, admitting them and asking God for wisdom and help is a good thing. We are called to give Him all our worries and cares as He cares for us (1 Peter 5:7). It's called crisis intimacy. You're in this together.

3. **You'll keep heading in the same direction as a couple.** Unity is a good thing. Build according to His plan, maintaining a shared commitment toward a better marriage. Unless the Lord builds your house, you will labor in vain in building it (Psalm 127:1).

4. **You'll have a better chance of each of you staying close to the Lord.** A soft heart is a responsive heart. A sinful heart separates you from God. By keeping surrendered to Him, in prayer, you can more easily hear and do what He wants you to do as a partner, a parent, and a person. Hebrew 3:12 calls us to watch out for each other for "a sinful, unbelieving heart that turns away from the living God."

5. **You'll show love for your spouse as you pray with them and for them.** You know their needs and concerns. Love is lifting them to the Lord and, in so doing, carrying their burden with them (Galatians 6:2). Pray for your spouse.

6. **You'll enjoy the sense of being anchored to God with your lives.** There is something bigger going on than just the two of you. God is with you. He'll never leave you and knows all you are facing. Let Him be the anchor for your marriage's soul, firm and secure (Hebrews 6:19).

7. **You'll have a softer, more forgiving heart toward each other.** Face it. You can't expect God's forgiveness if you won't extend it to your spouse. Go to God either relationally connected or asking Him to help you reconnect. Since you can't play games with God, why not quit playing games with each other? In marriage, if you walk in the light of the Lord, you'll have fellowship with each other (1 John 1:7).

8. **You'll keep humble as people and as a couple on your knees.** We do need God to make sense out of life. Tell Him so. Fight your human nature that strives for independence from God. Remember, prayer is the two of you as creatures humbly kneeling together before your creator. He is sovereign.

9. **You'll defeat the enemy who wants to divide you.** Remember, he prowls around like a roaring lion looking for a couple to devour (I Peter 5:8). Through your sincere and alert prayers together, you unleash God's power in your lives and marriage. The enemy will have a far harder time to touch you with his schemes.

10. **You'll prevent your own divorce.** Research shows that couples with a shared faith and common spiritual values are amongst those who enjoy a longer, more satisfying marriage (see John Gottman et al.). Of couples that pray together daily, less than 1% of them have a chance of ever experiencing divorce (Gallup Poll by the National Association of Marriage Enhancement, 1997). Go figure. God does have a plan – pray together.

That old familiar saying still rings true: "A family that prays together stays together." Do it.

DISCUSSION STARTERS:

1. Why don't you and your spouse pray together? Share two or three reasons.

2. What are personal fears about praying with your mate?

3. Which of the ten benefits do you value the most? List two.

Chapter 26
How to Start Praying Together

Dr. Dave Currie

Remember, relational research shows that 92% of couples that call themselves Christians never pray together. There's a good chance that you may be one of those couples who don't. Yet, pause and say it slowly...*never pray together*...somehow it doesn't sit right.

Not to sound "holier than thou", but I have repeatedly benefited by praying with Donalyn. It's become a non-negotiable for us and a significant point of connection that we've been doing nearly every day since even before we were married. Yet, for so many couples that I talk to who want to pray together and know they should, can't just seem to get there.

Jesus put it this way: "For where two or three come together in my name, I am there with them," (Matthew 18:19-20 GNT). God is asking that we pray together. When a couple joins in prayer, God is there with them. That's a good plan. This might be a great visionary goal for prayer in your marriage:

> *Couple prayer is a husband and wife, who being honest with their God and with each other, join together regularly, in spite of their marital imperfections or personal brokenness, to humbly reach out to Him for strength, direction and perspective.*

They go to God as one. They want His will for their lives and family.

You might agree that it is a good thing to pray together, but making the step to start praying together takes intentional effort. Here is a boatload of my best suggestions on how to start praying together:

WHEN TO START PRAYING TOGETHER
1. **All the time.** We are told to *"pray without ceasing..."* (1 Thessalonians 5:17), thus to be continually ready and willing to pray. So yes, pray at mealtimes to keep the attitude of gratitude alive in your home. But also pray as a couple every day at a specific time that works best for both of you.

2. **In the tough times.** Pray together before you attempt to resolve any critical issue or are having a conflict seeking to have the Lord guide you in not only how you interact but in getting an agreeable solution. Pray during times of crisis in your lives and family. Take your concerns to Him.

3. **In the good times.** Pray after a good heart-to-heart talk about life, forgiveness or your marriage to "seal the deal" with God as your witness. Pray at pivotal times of celebration

and transition as a family like starting school, anniversaries, birthdays, moving into new homes, graduations, leaving home, etc. Thank God a lot for His goodness to you.

HOW TO START PRAYING TOGETHER

1. Agree to pray together daily for one month. Let this be your test run. Learn. Grow. Adjust.
2. Choose a selected time to pray each day that works best for the two of you.
3. Keep your prayer times short (five to seven minutes) and sincere (from the heart as best possible).
4. Take turns, alternating each day. You both don't need to pray, though you can.
5. Hold hands when you pray. Go to God as one, not in perfection, but with a soft heart toward each other and the Lord.

WHAT TO START WITH WHEN YOU PRAY TOGETHER

Sometimes I feel that I would just be asking God for things in my prayers, so I try to use the ACTS acronym: Adoration, Confession, Thanksgiving, Supplication. Jody shred her perspective on this in Chapter 10.

1. **Adoration: Acknowledge how great God is.**
   a. Start by telling God what you love about him and focus on his amazing character before the problems of this world. Starting with adoration will build your faith and help your problems feel less destructive.
   b. Sounds like: God, you are so loving. You have created the world and everything in it. You know everything about me and you take care of my needs. You are worthy of my praise and adoration! I give my life to you again!

2. **Confession: Say sorry to God for when you fall short or mess up.**
   a. Confess your failures in life and marriage seeking forgiveness from Him and each other.
   b. Sounds like: God, I am sorry for how impatient I have been this week. I am sorry for not holding my tongue when I was angry and also for saying hurtful things to my spouse. Please forgive me and help me to apologize to my spouse as well.

3. **Thanksgiving: Share your appreciation for his goodness and blessings.**
   a. Rejoice together with answered prayer. Give thanks to the Lord for His goodness in your lives.
   b. Gratitude Prayers Sound Like these:
      - Thank you for hearing my prayers and answering them in your timing.
      - Thank you for answering me in your way, not even what I specifically asked for.
      - Thank you for knowing what is best for me.
      - Thank you for helping me say sorry to my spouse.
      - Thank Him for His on-going blessings you enjoy. Show gratitude.

4. **Supplication: Ask God for his providence in your lives.**
   a. Pray for your spouse: Pray specifically for each other. You know your spouse's world, concerns and pressures better than anyone else.

b. Ask God to keep your marriage strong; to help you to remain faithful to each other; and that together you will serve Him by touching the world around you.

c. Seek His will for guidance on decisions and direction for the family. Listen for His voice and prompting.

d. Pray for others: Reach out to God on behalf of others in your network. Lift up the needs of friends, neighbors, extended family, pastors, missionaries and whomever God brings to mind (health, finances, etc).

SPECIAL PRAYER IDEAS THAT WORKED FOR US

1. Good-bye Prayer: For years, we have prayed for those who have visited in our home at our front door when they are leaving.

2. Alarm Prayer: I set five alarms on my watch to go off every day for over six years to prompt me to pray more for my wife and four children. Face it. I am no prayer warrior. As a dad, I needed all the help I could get to be more faithful at holding up my family in prayer.

3. Accountability Prayer: For over thirty-three years now, I have met with another man to hold me accountable to what I believe God telling me is most important in my life. We pray every week for each other and our families.

4. Family Celebrations: We hold a family prayer time for moments of celebration and transition, like graduations, new homes, pregnancies, babies and new jobs – even Thanksgiving, Christmas and birthdays.

5. Fasting Prayer: Donalyn and I have practiced fasting for focused times of seeking God together on critical decisions and life transitions.

Well, there you go. I have tried to be really specific and practical in my help. Get brave and get started praying together tonight. Just start doing it!

DISCUSSION STARTERS:

1. Reread the GOAL for couple prayer below. Share what you like about it:
    Couple prayer is a husband and wife who, being honest with their God and with each other, join together regularly, in spite of their marital imperfections or personal brokenness, to humbly reach out to Him for strength, direction and perspective. They go to God as one. They want His will for their lives and family.

2. From the specifics given on how to get started – talk through and agree on your plan to begin consistently praying together.

3. Which of the special prayer times or ideas would you like to incorporate into your lives and marriage?

Chapter 27
Shut Up and Be Kind

Jody Wandzura

The counselor wished he could yell, "Shut up and be kind!" He said it would help couples solve their problems quicker if they could just be nice to each other! Kindness is the central backbone of any great friendship. Without it, a genuine relationship likely doesn't exist. Kindness softens responses and keeps things warm. If you want a marriage you enjoy, you need kindness in your daily interactions.

There are three levels of kindness, which we have titled Professional, Mutual and Relational.

Level 1: Professional Level
The Professional Level demonstrates basic kindness. It represents being an outstanding citizen with good manners and a polished demeanor. It's common courtesy. Imagine walking into a professional office building. You hold the door for the person behind you. They thank you. You say "Good morning" to a co-worker passing by. You walk up to the elevator and insist that the other person goes in ahead of you. They ask what floor they can push for you. You smile and thank them. As you leave the elevator, you accidentally cut someone off. You quickly apologize, let them go ahead of you and wish them a nice day. This way, everyone is polite, courteous and acts professionally. Here are the summary requirements.

☐ Polite: Use please and thank you consistently.
☐ Patient: Listen to the end of their message without interrupting.
☐ Positive: Be thankful and grateful in your everyday disposition.
☐ Peaceful: Sincerely say sorry and apologize if you are rude.

Sometimes, we have this type of kindness around complete strangers more than we do around our own family. This basic level of positive treatment needs to be employed even in everyday life with people in our network. Being polite, positive and patient prevents you from being mean or starting an argument. What a peaceful home it would be!

Level 2: Mutual Level
Once you have attained that first level of kindness, you can move on to the next one, the Mutual Level. The goal for this level is to make life better for each other. We need kindness in our eyes, words, actions and perspectives – the feeling of mutual goodwill.

I recall a difficult situation with a co-worker. We had known each other for quite a few years, had become work friends and she had confided in me many times. We finished a project together, and it was a job well done. She was supposed to be my friend, so I was surprised when she reprimanded me before our boss for something that didn't occur. She mockingly pointed out my mistakes, would not let me explain my side of the situation and wouldn't look me in the eye. She was aloof and careless with her words. I was caught off-guard and so hurt by how she slighted me that all I could muster were two words: "Be kind!"

This co-worker regularly demonstrated professional manners, but when trying to get the boss's approval, she threw kindness out the window. The Mutual Level requires more than just "being a nice person"; you must work to connect and think of others intentionally.

- ☐ Eye contact: Be welcoming and friendly with your eyes.
- ☐ Encouraging: Be caring and thoughtful with your words.
- ☐ Effort: Be willing to serve and be helpful with your actions.
- ☐ Empathetic: Take the perspective of others and understand their situation.

As a teenager, I generally lacked kindness; the only perspective I cared about was my own. I may have stayed like this, but I remember my dad saying through my slammed door, "Don't you dare hurt those you are supposed to love the most!" He hit me with the truth. He was right. I was treating my own family worse than anyone else. They were imperfect, but that did not excuse my cold looks, rude words, selfish disposition or harsh treatment.

That incident has impacted me well into my adult years. I have often thought about that encounter and have asked myself many questions about my kindness. Do I come across as a polite and warm person? Are my eyes welcoming? Are my words gentle? Are my actions caring? Are my thoughts empathetic? Do I show extra kindness to my spouse? My family? My friends? My co-workers? Asking myself these questions brought about a new awareness in my life.

Level 3: Relational Level

The final level is the Relational Level, which requires an intentional focus on slowing down, moving closer and connecting with affection toward your spouse and family. Imagine taking a warm blanket out of the dryer and wrapping it around yourself. That is the feeling of this level.

One Sunday at church, I looked across the room to see an elderly couple. She pushed him in his wheelchair, and they pulled up to their regular spot in the front row. She leaned in to listen to him and then proceeded to help him take off his raincoat. She got some things out of her bag and handed him a lap blanket. She was gentle, and he looked at her thankfully. When the singing started, she carefully took his hand and helped him stand. They continued holding hands for the full singing time. They leaned their heads together during prayer time and prayed for longer than most. This dear couple impacted me. Their kindness towards each other blessed me and inspired me to do the same. They are the perfect example of the Relational Level of kindness.

- ☐ Sweet: Use a warm tone when interacting.
- ☐ Slow: Be quick to listen, slow to speak and gentle in your response.
- ☐ Scooch: Lean into the conversation with both body posture and proximity.
- ☐ Service: Do not keep score of fairness, but look to serve the other.

This is the level that I need to work on as the years have progressed in my marriage! Instead of being a warm blanket, I sometimes act more like a wet towel. Too often, amidst life's busyness, my default list is sharp instead of sweet, speeding up versus slowing down, on-the-move trumps scooching closer and acting like the fairness police sometimes stops me from serving. Sometimes, I am too interested in my personal agenda, pointing out others' shortcomings or trying to make things equal. My husband even says that I sound like I want to start a fight. I don't *mean* to sound like this. I don't *want* to sound like this, so I definitely need God to help me with this level. Slow down. Take a deep breath. Say something sweet. Do something nice. Choose the warm blanket.

Kindness is underrated and underused but so needed. I Corinthians 13 has got it right: "Love is patient. Love is kind...it is not arrogant, rude, irritable or resentful." Marriage can always use more kindness.

DISCUSSION STARTERS:

1. Which trait(s) do you need to improve at the professional level? Discuss your answers.
   - Polite: Use please and thank you consistently.
   - Patient: Listen to the end of their message without interrupting.
   - Positive: Be thankful and grateful in your everyday disposition.
   - Peaceful: Sincerely say sorry and apologize if you are rude.

2. Which trait(s) must you enhance at the mutual level? Discuss your answers.
   - Eye contact: Be welcoming and friendly with your eyes.
   - Encouraging: Be caring and thoughtful with your words.
   - Effort: Be willing to serve and be helpful with your actions.
   - Empathetic: Take the perspective of others and understand their situation.

3. Which trait(s) must you develop at the relational level? Discuss your answers.
   - Sweet: Use a warm tone when interacting.
   - Slow: Be quick to listen, slow to speak and gentle in your response.
   - Scooch: Lean into the conversation with both body posture and proximity
   - Scoreless: Do not keep score of fairness, but look to serve the other.

Chapter 28
The Merging of Lives:
How Two Become One in Scheduling
Dr. Dave Currie

Our first fight was on the very first weekend home after our honeymoon. I had made an assumption – foolish, single-minded me – that Saturday morning was still my own, so I went water-skiing with the boys. I hadn't shared my plans with my new bride. Donalyn had assumed we'd be spending the day together – just the two of us. Her disappointment was huge. So it began...the complicated journey of two becoming one – starting with our schedules!

Scheduling complexities don't just go away. Just this past year, nearing five decades into our marriage, we still have a problem in getting it right. I decided I needed to go into work for a half day on a Saturday as I had gotten behind that week with a heavy load of crisis marital counseling. Donalyn thought that we'd be spending the whole day together. Neither of us had confirmed anything with each other for the day. We had both made assumptions.

Assumptions are deadly, as you will find out. I headed out quite early that morning while she was still asleep. Later that morning, I was met with a rather icy phone call with her disappointment leaking out all over. Working extra hours wasn't the problem; not communicating our plans and expectations for the day – mine to her and hers to me – was the issue.

The never-ending attempt at merging our lives continues...

This joining of two lives in marriage is a gradual process that takes a ton of selflessness. Trying to blend your life schedules requires practice, clear communication and often comes through trial and error. I have made so many errors. I am reminded of the one time in my self-centered preoccupation, I actually drove away from church leaving Donalyn and the kids there, thinking they had received a ride home with another family. Oops...arriving home to an empty house. Funny now; not so then.

Too often, when two people join together in marriage, they don't realize that both think that their plans and desires will usually win out over the joint plans. Wrong. Your life is NOT your own once you get married. Marriage is joint living, planning, negotiation and compromise. It is the full and intentional sharing of lives, starting with the schedule! If you don't communicate well about the details of your schedule, it will lead to greater and unnecessary frustration between you. Your mate cannot read your mind. Don't assume merging will happen easily! Checking with each other on all plans – his, hers and ours – needs to become the new norm.

You must target better clarity in communication, a means of confirming your decisions and then an agreed method for keeping track of those ever-changing, duo calendars. Most can share calendars on their phone. It will require great patience to successfully join your worlds. The following principles will guide you toward a healthy integration of both your lives and your schedules. Talk them through as a couple.

Great Principles on Merging Schedules:

1. **Set the Stage With These Core Principles**
   a. Inclusion: Make no commitments to outside people or activities without first confirming with your mate. Taking time to make joint decisions on couple or individual opportunities shows respect and equal voice in life. Very wise.
   b. Fairness: Be sure that both spouses have the same right to freedom and schedule control. Work-related deadlines and child-care demands can affect discretionary time. Communicate often so things remain fair and both people feel valued and equal.
   c. Priorities: Be sure that your personal and combined schedules have left enough time to keep your marriage a priority. Agree upon an adequate amount of time together before justifying more time apart.

2. **Observe the Rules for Scheduling**
   a. Be On-time: When confirming a time of meeting with your spouse (or others), agree on a specific time and then do your best to show respect by keeping to it. Both of your schedules are equally important. Come to an agreement about being on time for activities and appointments. What does being late mean? How will you face it together? One spouse may naturally be more time-conscious.
   b. Communicate Delays: If your plans change, you are held up or you have to cancel, let your spouse know as soon as possible. This is just common courtesy. You also need to apologize for changing the plans (especially on late notice as it has inconvenienced the other person). Text on minor changes – like being even a few minutes late. Call on more major changes of plans.
   c. Occasional Exceptions: Be patient and understanding with oversights as we all make mistakes. If you are the person who has made the mistake, never make excuses – just share the reason followed by an apology. You need to make the necessary adjustments so that you don't repeatedly make that same mistake again. It is disrespectful.

3. *Set a Time for Scheduling*
   a. Meeting: Have a weekly planning meeting for fifteen to twenty minutes on an agreed evening to navigate or negotiate through the following week's schedule. Be intentional about this! Example: Weekly plans discussed Sunday nights at 9:30 pm.
   b. Responsibilities: Plan what is going to get done when. You should have already divided responsibilities such as chores, childcare and specific errands, but occasionally you will need to coordinate who will do what based upon any scheduling clashes.
   c. Review: Take thirty seconds to summarize and agree on each scheduling decision to consider how it will impact the rest of the calendar. This will lead to fewer misunderstandings. You may need to ask for help or a change in the responsibility schedule for that day/week.

4. **Create a System of Scheduling**
   a. Shared Calendar: Create a shared calendar for all family and couple activities and plans, whether written or online. To keep each other fully aware of your separate activities should be assumed. Give access to each other's work and personal schedules. Each has a right to know the whereabouts, the associates and the activities of their spouse.
   b. Face Frustration: Talk through your current stresses with your schedules now and look for ways to compromise, accommodate and better connect each other's worlds.

Remember: God Is Your Best Guide in Scheduling Unity

Finally, it is wise to regularly commit your life's plans and marital schedule to the Lord in prayer together. He ultimately knows what is best for you. Take both your decisions and frustrations to Him. Let the following wisdom help shape your thinking. Look at these classic Scripture that will guide you on this:

- Proverbs 16:3 – "Commit to the Lord whatever you do, and he will establish your plans."
- Proverbs 19:21 – "Many are the plans in a person's heart, but it is the Lord's purpose that prevails."
- Romans 8:28 (TLB) – "And we know that all that happens to us is working for our good if we love God and are fitting into his plans."
- Philippians 2:3-4 – "Do nothing out of selfish ambition or vain conceit. Rather, in humility value others above yourselves, not looking to your own interests but each of you to the interests of the others."

Marriage is the merging of two lives, not the canceling of one. Work together for the prioritizing of your relationship. Focus on a fair merger. Enjoy equal voice. Communicate more. Hear each other out with respect. Pray about the merging of your lives. Remember, you'll never regret putting your marriage and family first.

DISCUSSION STARTERS:

1. Identify three current scheduling stresses you are having and set a time to talk about them to gain perspective and unity.

2. Apologize where you may have been selfish or careless with your spouse's life and schedule. Start fresh with each other.

3. Agree on what ideas here you'd like to implement. Suggest two each.

Chapter 29
Honeymoon Hints:
Clarifying Expectations
Jody Wandzura

Months and months of planning and preparation have gone into having the most beautiful, dream-come-true wedding day. Ceremony, vows, guest lists, flowers, dress, cake, centerpieces, DJ, and food have all required hundreds of decisions. The countless hours of precise details have all been worth it!

As the wedding day concludes, most men have already jumped in their mind to the anticipated evening at the hotel. What a performance it is going to be! He is excited for wild sex all night. His body is like a revving engine. He can't wait to get things going! He has big plans for them and even remembered to bring condoms. What a guy!

On the other hand, for many women, they are still in the moment, ensuring all the details unfold correctly right to the end. It has been incredible, but with so many people, decisions and stress leading up to their perfect day, she can't wait to get to the hotel and crash! Maybe she could soak in a hot bubble bath – perhaps they could even do that together. Then, they can give each other a back massage if she has the energy. She packed some massage oil and candles. That will be nice! Maybe they could have a romantic dance together to soft music. Hopefully, he has the perfect playlist all ready to go. Then, they collapse into bed, holding one another close and fall asleep in each other's arms. They have the rest of their lives to enjoy one another sexually, so why should they force it after a long, exhausting day?

Hmm...clearly different expectations.

After counseling many engaged couples in dating, sexuality, and marriage, we have realized the need for intentional communication, education and planning for the night after the wedding. We specifically created this chapter to discuss apprehensions and expectations to prepare for a great experience that both will mutually enjoy and cherish.

Apprehensions
Every person has their own sexual background which shapes fears, expectations and concerns. If a person has a variety of sexual experiences, their perspective will be different than someone who has waited to have sex. Regardless of your history, both may come with concerns and even baggage, so you need to have meaningful conversations with your fiancé about your wedding night and about sex in general.

If you trusted God's plan and committed to purity before you got married, sex will be a special gift that you can finally give to your spouse. The more you have saved, the more there will be to share. So, this is why you need to discuss what you want on your first night. Do you wish to try everything in the first twelve hours? Or are you planning on taking things slowly and enjoying each aspect over time?

For those who did not wait, sex outside of marriage is often a selfish act of what feels good for you, usually due to a lack of communication and commitment. Your conversation may need to be about starting your married sex life with a Godly perspective. First of all, God is all about forgiveness and new starts, so spend some time in prayer, recommitting your new sexual relationship to Him. Secondly, to ensure that sex is mutually enjoyable, you may need to discuss these essential topics along with your preferences, dislikes and what you wish your wedding night to entail.

> Inexperience: Our culture says you must have experience to be good at sex. We claim that inexperience and innocence are the greatest gifts you can give your spouse. You have the rest of your lives to gain proficiency together, and you save yourself from the baggage that comes from unhealthy sexual memories. How do you feel about your experience level?

> Comparison: Especially if your partner has been sexually active with other people, there can be anxiety to do with comparison. Will I be good at having sex (performance)? Is my body desirable enough (attractiveness)? What concerns do you have to do with comparison?

> Body image: Some people feel unsure or even dislike how their body looks when naked; therefore, they might prefer to have complete darkness initially or only a tiny candlelight. How do you feel about your body image? What could you do to get over insecurity? Do you compliment one another often (soft skin, big muscles etc.) to build positive self-esteem? What do you think about being naked together?

> Pain: The hymen (a small, thin piece of tissue at the opening of the vagina) will be broken when a woman first has sex. It is hardly noticeable for some women; it can cause discomfort and bleeding for others. After the hymen breaks, sex can be painful for up to a few days until it heals. You can choose whether to get a doctor to cut it ahead of time or do it naturally. Also, some women (often athletes or runners) have tight vaginal openings that may need to be gently and slowly stretched over time to enjoy sex without pain. What are your thoughts on this?

> Past abuse: It is imperative to go to counseling if you have been victim to any form of abuse – especially sexual abuse. It is not your fault what happened to you, but it is in your best interest to regain a healthy perspective toward sex going into marriage.

> Other questions? What other apprehensions do you have about sex?

Expectations

When it comes to the wedding night, your expectations are probably the most important conversation you should have with your new life partner. These discussions will look very different based on your sexual experience. This will be an ongoing conversation.

Your wedding night is going to be a time you will never forget. My husband and I still squeeze each other's hand whenever we drive by our honeymoon hotel. Therefore, we do not recommend spending your first night at your friends', parents' or relatives' house as this may create awkwardness. You should work to create your ideal setting but one that meets some criteria based on the following factors: location, lighting, music, attire, contraception, lubricant and food.

Location: First, you want the room to be beautiful as it sets the tone for a romantic first night together. Most hotels will let you go and view the honeymoon suite and compare it to a standard room. Usually, the honeymoon suite will have a soaker tub with special perks like chocolates and bath robes. On the other hand, consider how much of your budget you want to spend on this first night, especially since you may only be there for half the night, since your wedding will probably be late, and the drive there will also take some time. You may be going on a grand honeymoon, so the hotel on the first night does not need to be expensive. It all depends on what is important to you.

Lighting: Have you thought about special romantic lighting? Will you bring candles, or does your hotel not allow fire? Therefore, you will need to bring fake candles. Does your hotel room have a fireplace? Light dimmer? What about a disco ball or a strobe light? Who knows what you might choose! Discuss what is important to you in this area?

Music: What kind of music do you want on your honeymoon night? Will you use a wireless speaker, or is your phone speaker loud enough? Spend some time creating a playlist of all your favorite romantic songs together. Which songs are memorable to you?

Attire: Are you planning on having a special lingerie outfit for each other? Will she just have one, or will he get one also? Are you going to have only basic bridal showers or will you have a lingerie shower as well?

Contraception: It is a good idea to wait a few years after getting married before you start a family. Therefore, you must prepare if you don't want to get pregnant on your wedding night. Whether it is the birth control pill, different types of condoms, the birth control shot, or whatever prophylactic you choose, it is vital to become well-educated on your decision with the pros and cons of each option. Discuss the practical and moral implications of whatever decision you go with. This conversation should take place a few months before your wedding. You should come to agreement.

Lubricant: It is essential to have a type of vaginal lubricant like KY jelly or Astroglide for your wedding night. When a female is aroused, her body will naturally produce lubrication. There are many reasons why this might not happen on the first night, so preparation is critical. I even spoke to one couple who was allergic to the lubricant as it caused an unpleasant rash, so they switched to a different option .

Food: Have you done any thinking about refreshments and snacks? Some couples enjoy wine. Others might prefer champagne. Do you like chocolate? What about candy or other treats? My husband, Chris, thought it was a good idea to buy Gatorade! What refreshments and snacks will you choose?

DISCUSSION STARTERS:

1. Go through the topics listed above and discuss them to come to an agreement.

2. Each of you, take a moment to write an order of events you would like to do on your wedding night. When you finish, adjust the possibilities and agree on what should occur and when. Do not attach times to your schedule. Everything needs to be flexible.

3. Think about the final details.

   a. Will you get someone to set up your hotel room or do that yourself? Do you wish to have candles already lit, drinks on ice, music playing, fresh roses in a vase or any other special touches?

   b. What about your luggage to the hotel? Will you drop it off ahead of time? Or have it in your vehicle that you are going to drive there? Remember the following day's activities and what you will need to pack.

4. Do you feel that you have a healthy understanding of sex from a Christian perspective? Most people did not grow up with a family that discusses sexual concerns, so be sure that you read all the chapters in this book about sex and take the time to communicate on this topic maturely. In the future, continue to grow your knowledge of sexual intimacy by reading an entire sex book from a Christian perspective. My husband and I learned a lot from *Sheet Music* by Dr. Kevin Lehman.

Chapter 30
Loving With Your Eyes Wide Open:
Essential Engagement Questions
Dr. Dave Currie

Love is not only blind; sometimes it is plain stupid. Whether or not naïve to real issues while being in relentless pursuit to get married, too many people forge ahead in blissful euphoria. They not only turn a blind eye and avoid asking the hard questions, but they ignore sure-fire indicators of a questionable future. Sometimes your head needs to tell your heart to "SHUT UP!" It's okay to slow down and think about who it is you are marrying. It is actually really wise to be perceptive and discerning about your future primary relationship. That's where these engagement questions should come in.

Working through them honestly and thoroughly might reveal the need to delay the wedding!

When building a long-term relationship, my advice has always been to date at least through the four seasons of one year. You need time to get to know a person, because time enhances discernment. A variety of circumstances reveal character and tendencies. And if it's God's will that you should marry this person then for sure, you don't have to be in a hurry. God's will does not change – it only gets clarified. Time and different circumstances will only confirm whether or not stepping into marriage with this person is a decision that the Lord could bless. This line of reasoning isn't designed to question your decision but to confirm it.

It is through my experience in doing premarital counseling with over 750 couples, in performing 275 weddings and in counseling countless married couples in crisis (often because they didn't ask the hard questions early) that I bring this complete set of deep and discerning questions for you to ask each other. I believe the stronger the relationship and the more secure the person, the more welcoming they will be about going through the questions thoroughly and honestly.

It's good for both of you. It doesn't hurt to do these now whether engaged or already married. You either have nothing to hide or you are willing to own up to your shortcomings and share how you have handled them. Either way – it's about being honest. Lying about who you are will always come back to bite you. Remember Chapter 12 on "Coming Clean". Be honest. While it is natural to want to put your best foot forward in hopes that you might land this catch, sharing your history honestly is so critical. Your future spouse or new mate has to love you for who you are – warts and all. Honesty is not the best policy; it's the ONLY policy. Commit to it.

This chapter will help you in "Loving With Your Eyes Wide Open" so as to re-evaluate your engagement decision or start your marriage on a more solid foundation. I recommend that you be intentional about working through the following questions for greater discernment and increasing relational security. It would be wise to ask God together in prayer to guide you fully and honestly through this process.

Under each of the ten sections, there are a number of questions that need to be asked. Work through each one with both of you answering each question. No doubt, from time to time, other related questions will come up. Ask them too. The goal is honest disclosure. You should feel free to ask anything and shouldn't be afraid of your partner's defensiveness. Further, it might be wise to not try to do all the questions in one sitting. Spread it out over two to three talks. Best not to rush through it to just get it done.

1. **FAMILY OF ORIGIN:** What is the nature of your relationships within your family today? Are any of these relationships fractured? Parents? Siblings? Grandparents? Why? What have you done to overcome any brokenness? Did you grow up with love, affirmation and affection from one or both parents? Was there any physical, emotional or sexual abuse or harshness within your home? Do you value your family roots or would you rather distance yourself from your family of origin? Why? Did either of your parents display signs of mental health issues or addictions? What three words – positive or negative – would best describe your home life growing up?

   TALK HONESTLY...

2. **FAITH:** What is your faith journey? When did you accept Jesus Christ into your life? What is the nature of your family's faith? What have been other times of significant decisions or recommitments? How are you doing in your walk with the Lord now? Who has been the most influential person in the development of your spiritual life? What has caused the greatest growth in your walk with the Lord? What is the nature and consistency of your personal devotional life of Bible study and prayer? What is the regularity of your church involvement? How have you served in the church or in the community? What church are you thinking about being involved in? Are you committed to live and walk as a surrendered follower of Jesus Christ in your life and future marriage?

   TALK DEEPLY...

3. **FINANCES:** What are your views on money? How much debt are you currently in? What are you in debt for? Who do you owe money to? If you have debt, what are your plans for paying it off? Are you a spender or a saver? Are you given to impulsive buying or have a shopping addiction? What values have governed your current spending? What is good debt? Do you have any savings? What are your views on giving? Have you been tithing regularly? Have you ever been without work? Why? Do you lean more toward being casual about work or taking initiative regarding your opportunities to work? What are your financial goals regarding debt, savings and giving?

   TALK TRUTHFULLY...

4. **SEXUAL EXPERIENCE:** Please disclose all your sexual experiences up to this point in your life. What sexual abuse or trauma did you go through at the hands of others? What was the nature and level of your sexual activities in junior high, high school and college? What was the nature of your dating relationships and how involved sexually were you with each one? Did you have any one-night stands or merely sexual hook-ups? Were you ever involved in a rape or had a part in an abortion? Did you have any same-sex experiences? Did one or more of your parents have extramarital affairs that you are aware of? All these experiences shape your sexual love map – please be honest.

TALK WITH FULL DISCLOSURE…

5. **BOUNDARIES:** What are the friendship limits and boundaries that you have with the opposite sex now that you are in a committed relationship with me? What about relational and physical parameters with regard to time alone, affection and private conversations? What digital boundaries are wise and appropriate regarding texting, phone calls, emails or any other form of private messaging? Are you willing to give all your passwords to all devices and accounts? Are you willing and will you now make your phone or iPad available for scrutiny? Are you willing and will you now make your schedule, your whereabouts and your activities open to see? Agree on Relational Boundaries.

TALK WITH SURRENDER…

6. **PORN:** What has been the level of your pornographic involvement? When did you start watching porn? When was the last time you viewed any porn from any source? In between, how regular was your viewing? Was masturbation frequent with your viewing? What have you done to overcome it? Would you be willing to put a protection software (like Covenant Eyes) on all your electronics to filter any questionable content and to report your viewing habits to an accountability partner and to me?

TALK FORGIVEN AND WITHOUT SHAME…

7. **ADDICTIONS:** What habits have mastered you? What has been your emotional drug of choice in facing hard times? Have you had a problem with recreational drugs? What has been your experience with hard drugs? Have you ever over-used or been addicted to prescription drugs? What is your view and practice toward alcohol use? Do you have or have you had any eating disorders – anorexia or bulimia – and what have you done to overcome them? What has been your level of activity with gaming or gambling online and in person?

TALK WITHOUT ANY DENIAL…

8. **ODDS AND ENDS:** For these, it may be as simple as a yes or no. And if yes, just get them to explain further. Have you ever been involved in criminal activity? Ever been arrested? Hospitalized? Medicated? Any gang activity? Have you ever been fired from a job? Have you done any illegal activity? Been in any vehicle accidents? Any court cases outstanding? Any serious health issues? Have you had any operations? Have there been times of significant

stress, anxiety or depression? Is there anything else that if it came out later would in any way hurt me, break trust with me or cause me to regret a decision to proceed with this relationship?

TALK WITHOUT HOLDING BACK – THEY MUST LOVE YOU FOR WHO YOU ARE…

9. **CHILDREN:** What are your desires with regard to having children once married? How many? How soon? What will be important for you in raising your kids? What values do you want to teach them? What place will faith and church involvement play in the building of your family? Will one parent stay home for a season beyond the maternity or paternity leaves? Who will be allowed to babysit the kids? What do you feel about grandparent involvement, especially if there are complicated families of origin?

TALK HONESTLY AND HOPEFULLY…

10. **CHARACTER:** This is a big one. Many aspects reveal character. It's not about what people say about themselves and how they operate that counts. It's what they actually do! In this section, these questions are for you to ask yourself about the one you have been dating. Is there consistency with their words? Are they good with follow-through on their commitments? Do they make excuses justifying their oversight? Are they responsible? Do they do what they say they will do? Have you caught them in a lie? Do you find them defensive? Do they ever apologize? Do they tend to blame you for most problems? Have they asked you to do something that you know is wrong? Have they taken something that doesn't belong to them? What do their priorities seem to be? What is important to them? Do they have values that are clearly different than yours? Do you feel you can trust what they say? Do you feel safe and encouraged when around them?

After asking yourself these questions in private, what questions do you need explanation on? Ask them. Listen close for honesty, lack of defensiveness, ownership of mistakes and fair responses.

Personal Assessment of the Rightness of This Choice

Marriage is for life. This decision is critical. Having a full and honest discussion of these questions will bring clarification and comfort. You are good but you are loving with your eyes wide open. The answers to these questions can also bring concern and confusion. You are not good and you may be in a position to hold off on the wedding plans. Answer these questions below for yourself and your closest confidantes to discuss before addressing any concerns with your fiancé or new spouse.

1. What did you learn about your partner that you didn't know before?

2. What surprised you about the answers they gave you?

3. What topics do you feel you need to ask more questions about?

4. Do you have any doubts that they are telling you the whole truth on some issues?

5. How confident that you are making a good decision in marrying them?

6. Who would it be wise to talk to about any concerns you have?

7. What are your next best steps to take?

Meet the Authors

Jody Wandzura, MA in Leadership

Teacher – Coach – Speaker – Counsellor

Jody Wandzura is a fire-ball. Her passion for excellence in life showed early in university basketball where she became the top 3-point shooter in Canada while playing for the University of Calgary. She never stops – literally – as she has run 12 marathons to date.

After two Bachelor's degrees in Kinesiology and Education, she went on to earn a Master's in Educational Leadership focusing on equipping high school students and premarital couples in relationship education. She inspires teens by her example and deep love for them. She has been Athletic Director and Junior High teacher for 21 years. As a coach, she loves developing young women toward God's best in their life.

Jody is a sought-after speaker in her own right having spoken on relationships at FamilyLife's Weekend to Remember conferences, the Focus on the Family Canada tour, Women's Retreats and even speaking a dozen times at her home church. She has travelled with her Dad speaking at Parenting Conferences, Father-Daughter Retreats, Youth Conferences and Athletes in Action events. She has led and ministered on 14 Mission Trips – 4 with her Dad.

For fun, Jody plays in a women's soccer league with the best group of women in the world! She also enjoys going for outdoor excursions, thrifting adventures, and will never say "no" to a coffee a with friend.

Jody is married to her husband, Chris, for 23 years and enjoys her two teenagers, Mazy & Javen. She has dedicated her life toward equipping youth and young adults with God's principles on life, character and relationships. She is widely known for her vibrant, passionate faith that inspires others in following Jesus. Along with Chris, they developed a comprehensive premarital curriculum much of which is featured in this book, instructing over 25 couples toward *The Ideal "I Do"*.

Her life motto is to be "joyful, prayerful, and thankful." Her favorite verse is Colossians 3:23 *"Whatever you do work at it with all your heart as working for the Lord and not for others."*

Dr. Dave Currie, MA, Ph.D.

Speaker – Author – Educator – Therapist

Dr. Dave Currie is a relationship warrior. He directs **DOING FAMILY RIGHT**, a ministry inspiring people to follow God's blueprint for life and marriage. He leads two *Care Centres* overseeing 20 counsellors who coach on marriage and family with God's plan for life and the home.

Dr. Dave is a charismatic communicator and brilliant therapist empowering people with innovative and God-honoring advice that men respect and women trust. He holds two Master's Degrees in Counseling Psychology and Christian Education as well as a Ph.D. in Education focusing on Marriage and Family. He has spoken with many organizations including the Billy Graham Evangelistic Association, Insight for Living, Promise Keepers, Focus on the Family, Family Life and Athletes in Action.

Dr. Dave was host of the TV Talk Show *"Marriage Uncensored with Dave & Christie"* for 6 years producing 190 shows that grew to a viewing audience of ¾ million people weekly. He taught 10 years at Briercrest Bible College, was adjunct professor for 11 years at Columbia Bible College and pastored for 15 years in three locations: Centre Street Church, Calvary Baptist Church and Northview Community Church (a church of 4000). He also served as National Director of FamilyLife Canada for 8 years.

Dr. Dave has lectured on family and faith issues to a myriad of Vocational and Professional subcultures including Doctors, Chiropractors, Dentists, Educators, Police, Firemen, Business Leaders, Small Business Owners, Realtors, Pro Football Players, Members of Parliament, Pastors, Lawyers, Counselors, and Financial Planners as well as 1000's across all major denominations.

For fun, Dr. Dave has run 3 marathons, 4 Tough Mudders and enjoys playing hockey and golf. He bungee jumped at Whistler, whitewater rafted the Hell's Gate Canyon and summited Mt Baker- all with his daughter, Jody. He and his wife, Donalyn, have been married 50 years and have 4 married children and 13 grandchildren.

His Life mantra is – **Put God First – Life Goes Best.** His life verse is Phil. 1:20- *"I eagerly expect and hope that I will in no way be ashamed, but will have sufficient courage so that now as always Christ will be exalted in my body, whether by life or by death."*

APPENDIX

Listen and Watch Together to Improve Your Marriage

Go to DoingFamilyRight.com

The Doing Family Right podcasts and videos are listed below by the themes in the book. As well, many episodes of Dr. Dave's TV Talk Show, *Marriage Uncensored* are included in the resource list. There are over 100 audio/video resources to encourage your new marriage. Listen and watch together to deepen your relationship and to build a growing commitment to each other. By listening to Dr. Dave in person, you will gain great insight on each topic you have read in the book. Enjoy them to go deeper in your marriage.

PODCASTS: The Doing Family Right Podcasts are anchored by Dr. Dave Currie, the resident marriage and family expert, who has been hosting the show for over 10 years. He is joined by many great hosts and guests. Go to www.doingfamilyright.com/resources/podcasts to locate the DFR Audio Podcast that corresponds to the chapters and topics in this section. Podcasts are listed by number.

TV TALK SHOWS: For 6 years and over 185 episodes, Dr. Dave produced and hosted *Marriage Uncensored with Dave & Christie* while he was National Director of FamilyLife Canada. This marriage and family TV Talk Show aired each week nationally across Canada and much of the USA on the PBS network. With a broadcast reach that peaked at 165 million potential viewers, the show enjoyed a weekly viewership that grew to 750,000 people. It is recommended for you as a resource to both entertain and educate you to a better marriage as you enjoy many of the top experts in the world on the show.

Each episode of *Marriage Uncensored* has four segments in a 30-minute format with a set of interactive questions designed for couples to discuss to take their marriage deeper after each segment. Click on Part 1 of each show and you will be led to parts, 2, 3 and 4. Go to www.doingfamilyright.com/resources/tv-show/ to access the TV shows listed below by show title.

TEACHING VIDEOS: The Dr. Dave videos have been recorded online over the last 3 years to 60-80 men and women working hard on recovering from pornography, sexual or love addiction. He also covers relevant topics for your marriage. Go to www.doingfamilyright.com/regroup/teaching-videos/ to locate the DFR teaching video that corresponds to the themes and topics in this section. Videos are listed below by number and topic.

NOTE: There are scores of really helpful teaching videos and resources on **Porn or Sexual Addiction Recovery** for those wanting freedom in this area.

Go to DoingFamilyRight.com

Audio – Video Resources

MARITAL COMMITMENT:
1. Podcast 1: Ripe for the Picking
2. Podcast 21: Getting a great start in your Marriage
3. Podcast 37: Comeback Marriage: Keeping the Hope Alive
4. Podcast 43: The Laws of Relational Equilibrium
5. Podcast 63: Myths about Divorce and Remarriage
6. Podcast 68: Putting Your Spouse First and Foremost
7. Podcast 75: Setting Boundaries in Relationships
8. Podcast 97: Rebuilding Trust in Marriage
9. Podcast 120: The Power of Shared History
10. TV Show: Big Wedding – Little Marriage with Julie Baumgardner
11. TV Show: Close Calls: Closing the Door on Cheating with Dave Carder
12. TV Show: Divorce Remedy: Marital Satisfaction Guaranteed with Dr. Michele Davis
13. TV Show: Platinum Marriage: Priceless Commitment with Mark Gungor
14. Video 81: Accessing Marital Atmosphere
15. Video 92: The Power of Faithfulness
16. Video 151: Creating Relational Boundaries – Part 1
17. Video 152: Boundaries Part 2: Drawing a Hard Line

B. MARITAL COMMUNICATION:
1. Podcast 3: Do You Speak My Language?
2. Podcast 21: Getting a Great Start in Your Marriage
3. Podcast 46: Woodpeckers & Turtles: Do opposites Attack or Attract?
4. Podcast 105: Stay Connected When Work Calls You Away.
5. Podcast 112: Facing Depression in a Life and Marriage
6. TV Show: Communication: The Missing Link with Dr. John Van Epp
7. TV Show: Communication, Conflict and Closeness with Van Epp, Hawkins and Weiss
8. TV Show: Improving Your Marriage without Talking About It with Dr. Pat Love

C. MARITAL COMPANIONSHIP:
1. Podcast 2: Are you romantically Challenged?
2. Podcast 15: Learning to Gel: Building Life-long Friendship
3. Podcast 23: When a Spouse Forgets a Special Occasion
4. Podcast 32 – The Secrets of Happy Camper Dating
5. Podcast 44: Facing Your Spouse's Bad Days
6. Podcast 64: What Happens When the Butterflies of Love Die
7. Podcast 77: The Laws of Attraction
8. Podcast 130: The ABC's of Hugging
9. TV Show: Cracking the Code of Love with Dr. Sue Johnson
10. TV Show: The A.W.E. of Romance with Dr. Jim Burns
11. TV Show: The Differences between Man and Woman with Mark Gungor
12. TV Show: The DNA of Relationships with Dr. Gary Smalley
13. Video 184: The Secrets of Romancing Your Spouse

D. MARITAL CONNECTION:
1. Podcast 24: Marriage – Two people becoming on
2. Podcast 26: Moments that Matter: Connecting for Life
3. Podcast 84: The Acceleration of Connection
4. Podcast 89: Emotional Abuse in Marriage
5. Podcast 103: Personality Conflict in Marriage
6. Podcast 107: Why Emotional Closeness May Seem Impossible
7. Podcast 132: Drop Your Edge
8. TV Show: Hold Me Tight: The Emotional Dimension of Love with Dr. Sue Johnson
9. TV Show: Take Back Your Marriage with Dr. Bill Doherty
10. TV Show: The Secrets of Happily Married Men with Dr. Scott Haltzmann
11. TV Show: The Secrets of Happily Married Women with Dr. Scott Haltzmann
12. Video 119: The Self-Expression Window
13. Video 128: Understanding Husbandhood

E. MARITAL CONFLICT RESOLUTION:
1. Podcast 4: Rules of Engagement: How to Have a Fair Fight
2. Podcast 10: To forgive or not to forgive
3. Podcast 74: The Folly of Unforgiveness
4. Podcast 88: the Drag of Friction – Conflict Resolution
5. Podcast 132: Coming Clean
6. TV Show: Love Without Hurt with Dr. Steven Stonsy
7. TV Show: Why are You So Defensive with Dr. Steven Stosny
8. Video 31: Forgiveness Understood
9. Video 51: Making Amends
10. Video 63: The Anatomy of Forgiveness
11. Video 74: When God Forgives, He Really Forgives
12. Video 75: Learning to Forgive Yourself
13. Video 76: Learning to Forgive Others

F. MARITAL CLOSENESS:
1. Podcast 7: Sex Strike: How To Face Picket Lines In The Bedroom
2. Podcast 20: Overcoming Pornography in a Life and Marriage
3. Podcast 27: Sexual Intimacy in Marriage
4. Podcast 29: Overcoming the Effects of Childhood Sexual Abuse in Marriage
5. Podcast 47: Determining Sexual Variation in Marriage
6. Podcast 50: Securing Freedom from Pornography
7. Podcast 76: Sex Gaps – Finding Regular Intimacy in Marriage
8. Podcast 91: The Passion of Combustion: Sex in Marriage
9. Podcast 110: Understanding Lasting Marital intimacy
10. Podcast 129: Intimacy Roadblock: Overcoming Sexual Barriers in Marriage
11. TV Show: Sexual Issues Show with Eryn-Faye Frans
12. TV Show: High Speed Intimacy with Dr. Doug Weiss
13. TV Show: Sex: Now You're Talking with Dr. Gary Smalley
14. TV Show: The Sex-Starved Marriage with Dr. Michele Davis

15. Video 22: God, Sex and Relationships
16. Video 43: The Warning of Sexual Unfaithfulness
17. Video 108: Can Passion and Purity Co-exist?
18. Video 132: Coming Clean
19. Video 169: Putting God First in Your Passions
20. Video 189: God's Plan for Intimacy

G. MARITAL CONVICTIONS:

1. Podcast 11: Growing together spiritually
2. Podcast 19: What Happens when a couple prays together
3. Podcast 31: What Accountability Can Do for Your Life and Faith
4. Podcast 90: Family Missions: Serving Together
5. Podcast 94: The Difference of Faith in Marriage
6. TV Show: Soul Cravings: The Spiritual Dimension of Marriage with Erwin McManus
7. Video 47: Spiritual Growth as a Couple
8. Video 82: What Does God in a Marriage Look Like
9. Video 121: Experience the Power of God in your Life
10. Video 88: The Anatomy of Accountability
11. Video 181: His Way or My Way
12. Video 191: How Your Life in Christ Develops

H. MARITAL CONCERNS:

1. Podcast 8: When In-laws become Outlaws
2. Podcast 12: Merging Busy Lives and Schedules
3. Podcast 16: Beginning Steps of Financial unity
4. Podcast 17: Going Home for Christmas: Pressures and Problems
5. Podcast 38: Health and Fitness in Marriage
6. Podcast 67: Money in the 1st Five Years of Marriage
7. Podcast 71: Technology's Attack on Marriage: Finding Digital Boundaries
8. Podcast 79: The Gravity of Baggage
9. Podcast 100: What's Your Cell Phone Doing to You?
10. Podcast 104: Restoring the Peace in Extended Family Disputes
11. Podcast 111: Dealing with My Past before God, Spouse and Myself
12. Podcast 116: Getting Your Marriage Out of Debt
13. TV Show: Hope for a Collapsing Economy with Brad Willems and Eryn-Faye Frans
14. TV Show: Making More Money on Less Mistakes with Tim Cestnick
15. TV Show: Secret Wounds: When Your Soul Needs Healing with Drs. Tom & Bev Rodgers
16. TV Show: Will You Ever Get It Right: Balancing Work & Home with Mike Vogel
17. Video 32: Facing Your Soul Wounds
18. Video 168: Putting God First with Your Possessions

Yes... Book 2 in this series is set to go to press in the summer of 2024.

The Ideal *"I Do"*

Pursuing the Marriage You'll Love
Book 2: **Lasting Long**

By Dr. Dave Currie & Jody Wandzura

The Ideal "I Do" Series is designed as an ongoing resource like a new marriage owner's manual. Book 1: **Building Strong** is targeting pre-marriage preparation and Book 2: **Lasting Long** for newlyweds. We encourage the completion of the 2nd book to keep building strong to last long.

Why not first celebrate the completion of Book 1 – **Building Strong** – by going out and celebrating on a date! Then, dig in to Book 2 – **Lasting Long.**

Lasting Long of **The Ideal *"I Do"*** series is solidly built on the foundation of Book 1. You'll find it is designed to continue the marital growth toward pursuing the marriage you'll love. It is ideal for strengthening your new relationship in the first 5 years of marriage.

Again, the same engaging format will teach you, challenge you and guide you on more of the critical and practical issues for a marriage that not only last long but is one you want to be a part of.

Choose to go deeper toward a truly 'epic' marriage. Get Book 2!

Behind You All the Way,

Dr. Dave & Jody